DR. LESLIE M. DILLARD

The BLACK CHURCH And SOCIAL INJUSTICE

HOW DID WE GET HERE?

FOREWORD BY
JOSHUA D. HENSON, PH.D.

The Black Church and Social Injustice: How did we get here?

Copyright © 2023 by Dr. Leslie M. Dillard

ISBN: **979-8-9872196-2-1**

Published by:
Concise Publishing
2474 Walnut St. #105
Cary , NC 27518
www.ConcisePublishing.us

DEDICATION

To my parents, Lloyd and Barbara Dillard. Education was always an important part of my upbringing and you both modelled that for me. I appreciate your push and your prayers. Mom, you prophesied this degree. You saw what God was doing all along. Thanks for not giving up on me. Dad, thanks for keeping me abreast of the countdown. I love you for that. Although you are no longer with us, you let me know that you were proud of me.

To Dashe Hilson, my best friend. I know I got on your nerves more than a little bit! You pushed, pulled, prayed, advised, fussed, and encouraged me to do what God called me to do. Thanks for being that shoulder to cry on and believing in me when I didn't believe in myself. You truly are the epitome of Proverbs 27:17, "As iron sharpens iron, So a man sharpens the countenance of his friend" (NKJV).

ACKNOWLEDGMENTS

First, I would like to acknowledge Jesus Christ as my Lord and Savior. Without Him, I am nothing. He promised me He would provide all my needs, and He did. He executed His plan flawlessly, even when I tried to sabotage it. Thank you, Jesus, for always being faithful.

Next, I would like to acknowledge the Dillard, Briscoe, Moore clan. There is nothing like family. I love you all dearly and am grateful you did not allow me to fall by the wayside. To my brother Lloyd, you kept me laughing when I wanted to cry. To LaDara, Paul, Cindy, Marc, Liz, Marisol, Aquilla, Devin, and Crystal, the random calls and texts came right on time. Family Bible study kept me focused and grounded. Thanks for making sure I showed up. To Aubree, God has a plan for you! Never forget who you are! To Ashton, thanks for the hugs and kisses you send me; TT loves you.

Regent faculty: Dr. Henson and Dr. Serrano. You pushed me beyond what I thought was even possible. Thank you for the challenge – I am better for it.

My SBL classmates: Autonnette McLaughlin and Jannine Bell. You have no idea the impact you have had on my life. Jannine, I watched you battle COVID and keep up with the kids' activities without missing a beat. Autonnette, I cannot say enough about how you persevered. We made it! "D" still comes before "M," though! Thank you for all the assistance and words of encouragement along the way. Yall rock!

My spiritual leaders and mentors: Bishop Eugene Reeves, you got me into this thing. Thanks for not allowing me to run from my call. To Prophet Rozena Johnson and Dr. Donna Ferguson. Yall hurt my feelings in the most positive way possible. Thanks for not allowing me to wimp out and telling me it is time to grow up and take my rightful place.

To Pastor Susan Marshall and my SUMC family: You allowed me to test theories, write about our exploits as a church, listened to numerous briefs and theoretical ideas, taken multiple surveys, and put up with my pontification on how important the Greek and Hebrew are in context. I know I got on your nerves. However, without you, this would not be possible. Thank you for your prayers and for making yourselves available as guinea pigs for training experiments and deep conversations about the direction of our church. None of the reports I had to write would have been possible without Still Useable Ministries Church! Thank you, Pastor Marshall, for allowing me access to your leaders and your congregation.

To my friends, LaWanda Holliman, Cotina Reynolds, Antionette Adams, and the King's Kitchen, thank you for the prayers and words of encouragement. Prayer does change things, and I appreciate your diligence in staying on the wall.

FOREWORD

There is little doubt that American society is at a crossroads with rampant secularism and significant cultural shifts transforming the way Americans view the family, the Church, and the role of faith in the public space. While many thoughts may come to mind as we consider the current state of American society, there is one issue that has plagued us for centuries: racism and social justice. Four hundred years after the first slaves arrived on the shores of Virginia, we continue to wrestle with the ramifications of the darkest period in our history. Have we made great strides? Yes. However, when words like Rodney King, Ferguson, and George Floyd transcend the proper names of individuals and cities to become historical and cultural moments, it becomes clear that America's racial problems are real and pervasive.

In a speech at the Conference on Christian Faith and Human Relations in Nashville, TN on April 25, 1957, Dr. Martin Luther King challenged the Church to become leaders "in strong Christian social action" as he called us to shift our thinking: "In dealing with the race problem our thinking is so often anthropo-centric rather than theocentric…The Church must re-mind men, once more, that God is the answer, and that man finds greater security in devoting his life to the eternal demands of the Almighty God, than in giving his ultimate allegiance to the transitory eva-nescent demands of man." When it comes to racial relations, I have operated under the principle that racism is an evil that must be identified and eradi-cated, racial discrimination is a system that must be challenged and corrected, and racial ignorance is in-terpersonal and must be confronted and educated. Only the Gospel of Jesus Christ provides the answer to the evils of racism: Jesus Christ's victory over sin. However, His Church has been created to be a king-dom of priests (1 Peter 2:9) who are in the world but not of the world (John 17:16). We—the Church—are God's voice to a broken, sinful world. But how do we do it?[1]

In her book *The Black Church and Social InJustice*, Dr. Leslie Dillard answers the call of Dr. King and tackles the question of the role of the church in so-cial justice reform. At this point, you may be won-

[1] Martin Luther King, "The Role of the Church in Facing the Nation's Chief Moral Dilemma," https://kinginstitute.stanford.edu/king-papers/documents/role-church-facing-nation-s-chief-moral-dilemma-address-delivered-25-april.

dering why Dr. Dillard focuses on the "Black Church" and may question why she would not write to the Church at large. There is a cliché in the Church that says: "Judgment begins in the house of God." This is derivation of 1 Peter 4:17 where the Apostle Peter pointed to the eschatological realities of the last days Church—what will be punishment for the wicked is purifying for the believer.[2] Essentially, the culmination of things—the Second Coming of Christ and the eradication of sin—begins with the purification of the "family of God" through suffering. So, why the Black Church? Because healing and transformation must begin somewhere. Dr. Dillard has chosen to speak to her family—the people she loves and serves—the leaders and congregations that make up the Black Church in America.

The Black Church and Social InJustice was written to be challenging, yet redemptive. Dr. Dillard not only asks the hard questions but provides meaningful, biblical answers. With the heart of a servant leader, Dr. Dillard walks her readers through narrative after narrative that teaches us that God's redemptive plan for humanity is, in the words of Dr. King Jr., both timely and eternal. On our way to eternity, the Church can change the world. So, what is Dr. Dillard's

---

[2] 1 Peter 4: 17

message to the Black Church? "Family, let's lead the way."

Joshua D. Henson, Ph.D.
Associate Professor of Leadership
Southeastern University

References

King, Jr., M. L. (1957, April 25). "The Role of the Church in Facing the Nation's Chief Moral Dilemma." *The Martin Luther King, Jr. Research and Education Institute.* https://kinginstitute.stanford.edu/king-papers/documents/role-church-facing-nation-s-chief-moral-dilemma-address-delivered-25-april

TABLE OF CONTENTS

PREFACE

hile this book was born out of work in a doctoral program, it has come to mean much more. As an ordained minister and teacher of the Gospel, I wanted to understand the role of the Black Church in battling the social injustice we are seeing today. Why has the church's engagement waned over the years since Dr. King led marches and preached inspiring sermons to right such egregious wrongs? How does the Bible address social injustice? How do church leaders fight against the constant bombardment of "isms" within the community they reside? The "isms", racism, classism, and sexism, cause conflict and feed the contempt we have for human beings not like us.

This book provides a look at Biblical justice and challenges the church to examine its response to the injustice we are witnessing today. It provides thought-provoking questions to help church leaders and their staff develop a strategy to engage. Senator John Lewis stated, "We have been too quiet for to long. There comes a time when you have to say something. You have to make a little noise. You have to move your feet. This is the time." *(At a 2016 House sit-in following* <u>the Pulse shooting in Orlando</u>*)*.

To finally realize Dr. King's dream, let us take heed to Senator Lewis' words, let's move our feet, let's get to work, we can no longer be silent and expect change to come. The black church must engage, and it must be now!

INTRODUCTION

Grandpa was the preacher, and grandma was the organist. There was no escaping life in the Black church as a child. Grandma and mama made sure my brother and I knew how to pray, and we were in church, not just warming a pew but involved in all activities. Participation was not an option from being an acolyte and the near misses of burning the church down to singing in the choir, reading scripture, and engaging in all youth programs.

As a military family member, my church experience as an African American child included many memberships in several churches across several denominations. My father was raised Baptist and became a Baptist minister, effectively making me a preachers' kid (PK). Mom was raised Methodist. As we traveled the world, we attended a combination of denominations under the Protestant umbrella. There were White churches and White preachers, gospel services with Black congregants, multicultural congregations, and non–denominational churches that influenced my faith and worship experience.

At the age of 17, I accepted Jesus Christ as my Lord and Savior. I was baptized at Fort Foote Baptist Church in Fort Washington, Maryland, where I was introduced to the Holy Spirit. Needless to say, my walk was not always straight and narrow. I became acquainted with the Black church as I waffled between faith and recklessness. It would only be a matter of time before God called me to become a leader in the very organization I ran from – the church. God has a way of moving you along in life on the path He has set for you, no matter how many times you take a detour or walk away in blatant disobedience. He brings you back to what He called you to.

Mom taught me to love God, my neighbor, and myself. The concept of hate, racism, or bias on any level was not a part of my life until it was. Judgment based on the color of my skin and my gender was quite the reality check, especially in the Army, an institution dedicated to fighting for the rights of all. Am I an angry Black woman? No, but I could be but for the love of God.

How Did We Get Here?

Hate and injustice have been a part of our world since the very beginning. Satan's hubris and his ejection from heaven seeded a deep hatred of God and man. As a result, Satan's deception in the Garden of Eden cemented the downfall of man, and here we are today, dealing with the seeds of hatred and the deeply rooted injustice that grows from those seeds. We tend to deal with tree branches. We prune and cut back White supremacy, hate, bias, inequity, inequality, and injustice, seemingly unaware that the more we cut back, the more they grow. We never attack the root of the problem with any absolute conviction. Many acknowledge America's sins of colonialism, slavery, and racism. Still, there are just as many that deny that this nation's founders destroyed the indigenous population already residing here before European settlers arrived. Some saw nothing wrong with slavery and deny that there are no racial issues in the United States of America. So, why were we surprised when, on January 6, 2021, acts of violence graced the United States Capitol steps? That action, designed to disenfranchise votes cast by people of color to assert the rights of those who contend they are the privileged. Inflammatory speech and rhetoric stoked the flames of an already raging fire, inciting racial tensions that continue to percolate below this nation's surface. Why do we care more about the institutions that symbolize the country more than we care about the human beings that make up the institution? Violence has been part of the Black (African American) experience since arriving on American soil in Jamestown, Virginia, on August 20, 1619. America's silence signals its complicity in acts of violence against people of color. This nation will continue to bear the fruit of the tree called racism until there is repentance by the oppressor and forgiveness by the oppressed.

"We have come so far" is a statement used when we do not want to confront the truth in front of us. This statement is used when we want to feel good about any progress made toward righting a nation's wrongs. However, it remains a testament that people of color continue in oppression. The proof, they say, is in the pudding. Yes, America has made strides in addressing some of the injustices of the past. But what does it say that 33% of White practicing Christians say there is nothing the church should do in response to America's 400 plus year history of injustice against Blacks, and 27% do not know what the church should do.[1] How will we ever kill the root when 60% of White Christians see no role for the church in addressing racism? How do we make progress in an institution where 11:00 a.m. on Sunday (even in the Back church) is America's most segregated hour?[2]

---

[1] Group B, "Most Black Adults Say Religion & the Black Experience Go Hand in Hand," https://www.barna.com/research/sobc-2/.

[2] "The Martin Luther King, Jr., Research and Education Institute | https://kinginstitute.stanford.edu/.

The Black church has always been a place of refuge and strength for oppressed people. From the praise houses of old to today's edifices, the Black church is foundational to the Black community, the epicenter, if you will. The term "the Black church" evolved from the phrase "the Negro church," the title of a pioneering sociological study of African American Protestant churches at the turn of the century by W.E.B. DuBois. In the early days of the church, White Christians allowed Blacks to worship in White churches, albeit at the back or in the rafters. Suffice it to say that Black Christians in White churches did not work. Some individuals and even some churches recognize the depravity of Christian racism, so drastic a reform was nowhere on the agenda of the White church"[3]. As a result, Blacks separated from the White church. Richard Allen, an ex–slave, established the African Methodist Episcopal Church (AME), the first independent Black denomination in Philadelphia, in 1815. Mother Emmanuel was founded a year later, in 1816, in Charleston, South Carolina.

For African Americans, the politics of slavery, segregation, and Jim Crow wreaked havoc on any real opportunities to advance. The concept of race is a relatively recent development. Only in the past few

---

[3] Andrew Billingsley, *Mighty Like a River* (Oxford University Press on Demand, 1999).

centuries, largely due to European imperialism, have the world's people been classified along racial lines. Slavery was the result of a growing demand for laborers on plantations. After Indians and immigrants were ruled out, Africans became the prime commodity for slavery.[4] The impact of emancipation on southern culture energized a wave of violence and institutionalization of racist policies across the South is still felt today.[5] Given the current state of events in America, it must be acknowledged that these attitudes continue to be prevalent across the nation today.

The current condition for Black America was instigated by policies enacted during the Nixon and Reagan presidencies.[6] Researchers suggested a need for the Black Church to facilitate change. "The unity and commitment that many Black Church leaders exhibited during the civil rights movement is absent today at a time when African American communities need dedicated and inspired leadership to address injustice and inequality, poverty, mass incarceration, rac-

---

[4] Alexander, M. (2010). *The New Jim Crow.* New York: The New Press.

[5] Avidit Acharya, Matthew Blackwell, and Maya Sen, "The Political Legacy of American Slavery," *The Journal of Politics* 78, no. 3 (2016): 621-641, accessed May 22, 2023, doi: 10.1086/686631.

[6] T. A. Dutton (2007). Colony Over-the-Rhin. The Black Scholar, Vol 37, Number 3, 14-27.

ism, and crime."[7] If the Black community is to progress in social activism, the Black Church must engage.

The emergence of activist groups such as Dream Defenders, Black Lives Matter (BLM), and the Black Youth Project 100 occurred due to frustrations with continued social injustices related to race, sexual orientation, creed, and gender. There is a tendency to treat Blacks and Black culture as monolithic. Blacks are not a monolithic culture. This mindset leads to a perception that every Black organization or activist group originates from the Black church. To believe that these social activist organizations originated from the Black church is like saying the White evangelical church birthed the Proud Boys – simply preposterous!

So, where is the Black church in the equation? "The Montgomery bus boycott in 1955 was the catalyst for the Black consciousness movement."[8] The Black Church is ground zero for the Black community. As with everything else, "the civil rights movement was anchored in the Black Church, organized by both activist Black ministers and laity, and support-

[7] J. I. Clark, "Social Justice and Black Church Leadership: A Phenomenological Study," *Social justice and black church leadership: a phenomenological study* (Ann Arbor ProQuest LLC, 2014)

[8] E. C Lincoln and L. H. Mamiya, "The Black Church in the African American Experience," *Duke University Press* (1990): 165.

ed financially by Black church members."[9] Examining the views of Black clergy and the mission of the Black church, 55% of clergy conveyed their ministry is different because it is a Black denomination, and 63% stated the Black church does not have a different mission than White churches. Those that affirmed differences pointed to the "problems of racism in American society and the different social, economic, and cultural conditions of African Americans, which the Black clergy have to deal with."[10] A pastor from a rural church within the study stated, "Primarily, the Black Church has a responsibility to be involved in the total liberation of black personhood and help empower the Black community."[11]

Even with these observations, there was no sustained consistency across the multitude of Black churches to support or facilitate social justice discussions. There were Black churches across the South that became agents of social change as a result of the Civil Rights Movement. The Black church was the centerpiece of the Civil Rights movement that galvanized the African American community to elicit change across a nation. Given today's environment,

[9] Ibid.
[10] Ibid., 170
[11] Ibid., 171

is the Black church still influential and relevant in the fight against injustice?

Why this book?

For this nation to reverse course and overcome the current firestorm of injustice, the Black Church must take its place in leading and facilitating a course correction. The battle is not just about the state of the union; it is about the state of the nation's soul. United States citizens aspire to a peaceful existence. However, studying the scriptures, Jesus shared a parable about a widower who complained about a biased and unjust judge. The unjust judge received no peace until he finally relented to the widower.[12] The Black Church must be like the widower, regularly pointing out injustice and acting upon it until the desired outcome is achieved. Christ expects us as individuals to acknowledge our sin and repent. It is no different for a nation. The undercurrent of injustice will continue to erode this nation's foundation until America comes to grips with its sin.

The purpose of this book is to identify the role of the Black church in supporting justice reform and providing strategies to facilitate reconciliation and restoration across the whole ecclesia, White and

---

[12] Luke 18: 1-8, KJV

Black, as well as the nation. The national outrage at the deaths of African Americans at the hands of law enforcement has brought to the surface 400 years of systemic oppression and civil rights injustices. For many, the Black church is expected to address social inequities with the same zeal exhibited in the past. What will it take for the Black church to engage in social justice activism? This book is not written to disparage, minimize, or demonize anyone, any belief, or organization. It is designed to demonstrate and model how God dealt with injustice in the Old and New Testaments. This book will also examine how Dr. King modeled Jesus' nonviolent approach to achieve incredible social and political gains during the Civil Rights Movement of the 1960s.

Models of effectiveness cannot be examined without taking a look at how God prepared the leaders He chose to deal with injustices perpetrated on His people. In the Old Testament, we will examine Moses' rise to prominence and his interactions with Pharaoh as he demands Pharaoh to "let his people go." We will investigate Haman's attempted genocide of the Jews in the Book of Esther and her preparation to save her people. Finally, we look at how King David exacted justice on behalf of the Gibeonites in II Samuel 21 for persecution received under King Saul's rule.

The New Testament offers insight into how Christ addressed injustice. We will begin by examining Saul's obsession with oppressing the Jews and how Jesus' redeeming love turned a domestic terrorist into the most prolific writer of the New Testament. By today's standard, Saul (Paul) should have received the death penalty for his acts of terrorism toward the Jews. Jesus' sacrifice is the ultimate example of a people, you and me, not getting what we deserve as He endured the injustices that led to the cross. Finally, a look at the Book of Revelation, as we examine how God will deliver justice in the final judgment for all humanity.

Finally, we will go back six decades investigating how Dr. Martin Luther King Jr. used biblical principles and Gandhi's model of nonviolent activism to bring about political and social change within the nation. I was only four years old when the unthinkable happened – Dr. Martin Luther King Jr.'s assassination. I did not understand what assassination meant or even the impact his death would have on my life. As the world fell silent in disbelief at this heinous act, I watched as everything around me seemed to move in slow motion. My four–year–old brain was trying to grasp the magnitude of what happened. But even at four, I understood that this event was significant to little Black girls and boys like me. There was a shift in the atmosphere.

We cannot erase the past, but we can impact change for the future. We do not have to subscribe to the way it has always been. America walked away from God. He is calling us home. The blueprint for continued blessing and prosperity is found in the following scripture, "If My people who are called by My name will humble themselves, and pray and seek My face, and turn from their wicked ways, then I will hear from heaven, and will forgive their sin and heal their land.[13] As a nation, we must roll up our sleeves to correct the injustices perpetrated on the oppressed. America can still be the beacon of light God called it to be. The Black church can always make a difference by developing strategies to address injustices. We all have our roles to play. We must identify what they are.

God did not create us to hate or exhibit a bias toward one another. Hate is a learned behavior. God's commandment is to love Him and love our neighbors as ourselves. If we can learn to hate, then we most assuredly can learn to love. I pray that this book will generate conversations that will unite and not divide; that it will spark innovative and creative ways to address and heal old wounds. The church must take its place in leading change with love.

---

[13] 2 Chronicles: 7-14, NKJV

Background of the Problem

America's current social climate is a reminder that the fight against injustice is never far from the frontlines of national politics. Who addresses the plight of those marginalized because of race, gender, sex, ethnicity, and a whole host of personal and spiritual differences? The United States of America, founded on the principles of religious freedom, has, over time, backed away from the very principles the founding fathers espoused in the Declaration of Independence and the Constitution. There are many statements regarding religious diversity that can be applied to all areas of diversity. The nation must "reclaim the deepest meaning of the very principles we cherish."[14] So, what are the foundational principles of America? According to the Bill of Rights Institute, While not all-inclusive, it includes "due process, equality, freedom of religion, freedom of speech, press and assembly, majority rule with minority rights," to name a few.[15]

In reclaiming these foundational principles, the country must acknowledge diversity "is not simply tolerated but becomes the very source of our strength. There must also be a desire to "know more than we do about one another and contribute to the sound

---

[14] Diana L. Eck, *A New Religious America* (Harper Collins, 2001).

[15] "Bill of Rights Institute," accessed June 8, 2023, https:// billofrightsinstitute.org/.

and spirit of America.[16] It is evident in The Preamble to the Constitution that the founding fathers intended to establish justice. But what does this mean in the forming of a "more perfect Union?" Especially as today's news cycle reports chaos and mayhem related to racial injustice and inequity all across the country. What does scripture say about social justice against the backdrop of societal norms and expectations?

Most Americans believe in the American dream, the opportunity to become successful following a dream, ultimately becoming vertically mobile. However, it has been recognized that "the ordinary person has lived on the edge of starvation, slightly above subsistence level, with no rights and no justice."[17] The social problems that contribute to this state of being for the "ordinary" person are attributed to an economic system that favors the rich and powerful.

From a historical perspective, social justice is derived from the ancient Greeks and Romans. Under the influence of Plato and Aristotle, "the concepts used to interpret and organize political life were justice and equality."[18] Greek politicians and philosophers acknowledged the importance of justice; in the fifth

---

[16] Diana L. Eck, *A New Religious America* (Harper Collins, 2001).

[17] Ornstein, *Social Justice, History, Purpose and Meaning*, 541-548

[18] M Lane, *Ancient Political Philosophy* , E.N. Zalta (Stanford University : Stanford Metaphysics Research Lab , 2018).

and fourth centuries Before the Common Era (BCE), many of them also increasingly problematized it. [19] Biblically, the concept of justice is rooted in the tri-une God. "The Bible makes social justice a mandate of faith and a fundamental expression of Christian discipleship."[20] "Over the past few years, the rise of the term "social justice" among Christians has coincided with a growing level of misunderstanding, misuse, and misapplication of the term."[21]

"The notion of social justice is based on the Christian doctrine of helping less fortunate people—the weak, sickly, and oppressed.[22] Throughout the scriptures, Jesus demonstrated an abundance of love and care in teaching the disciples about justice. In Luke 6:37, Jesus teaches not to judge, so the disciples will not be judged.[23] Jesus told the disciples, "so whatever you wish that others would do to you, do also to them, for this is the Law and the Prophets."[24]Jesus admonished the scribes and Pharisees for neglecting

---

[19] Ibid.

[20] A. Taylor, "What Does Social Justice Really Mean? | World Vision," https://www.worldvision.org/blog/social-justice-really-mean.

[21] J Carter, "The FAQs: What Christians Should Know About Social Justice," accessed May 22, 2022, https://www.thegospelcoalition.org/article/faqs-christians-know-social-justice/.

[22] Ornstein, *Social Justice, History, Purpose and Meaning*, 545

[23] Luke 6:37, NIV

[24] Matthew 7:12, ESV

the "weightier matters of the law: justice and mercy and faithfulness."[25] Even before Jesus arrived, God dealt justly with His people in the Old Testament and conveyed just living, telling the Israelites to "keep justice, and do righteousness."[26] God's restoration of Job is another example of God's incredible just nature.[27]

It has been argued the Greeks believed citizens had certain rights and civic duties and could petition for those rights in the court. Cicero considered the "father of natural law for the modern era," warned the senate in Rome about greed and class warfare, which triggered inequity between them.[28] These ideas carried over into the establishment of the United States. However, the ideals written in the Declaration of Independence did not apply to everyone, and widespread social injustice occurred based on race, gender, class, and religion.[29] It was not until the 1960's that social scientists began to address the top-

---

[25] Matthew 23:23, ESV

[26] Isaiah 56:1, NKJV

[27] Job 42, KJV

[28] Ornstein, *Social Justice, History, Purpose and Meaning*, 545

[29] Christopher D. Merrett, "Social Justice: What Is It? Why Teach It?," *Journal of Geography* 103, no. 3 (2004): 93-101, doi: 10.1080/00221340408978584.

ic of justice.[30] Still, no formal name was assigned to the body of work at that time.

The mission of the church at large is to make disciples as directed by Jesus in Matthew 28:19. Does the Black church have an additional assignment to facilitate a discussion and act upon social justice issues? It has been suggested that even though there was an increase in activism during Jesse Jackson's run for president, "there remains a widespread tendency among some Black intellectuals and among many academics to completely separate religion from politics."[31] However, the current political climate has revealed that the evangelical agenda is not always God's agenda. "If White Christians acted more Christian than White, Black parents would have less to fear for their children."[32]

Given Black clergy's apprehension to comingle faith and politics, how does the Black church, the center of the Black community, address social justice issues and concerns? If we say we trust and believe in God, then the spirit must transcend the natural as we allow God to be God in helping society resolve socially unjust issues. Our responsibility as the

---

[30] Ornstein, *Social Justice, History, Purpose and Meaning,* 545

[31] E. C Lincoln and L. H. Mamiya, "The Black Church in the African American Experience," *Duke University Press* (1990): 163.

[32] Jim Wallis, *America* (Brazos Press, 2016).

church is to shine a light and expose injustice in the community while coming to the table with innovative and creative solutions. Even in the wake of today's efforts to suppress the Black and Brown vote, the Black church has a role to play. Studying the models of the Old and New Testaments as well as the Civil Rights Movement can be a launching pad for new opportunities to address old problems.

The Black church, not just a few Black preachers, but the church as a whole can once again lead the Black community in the hunt for social justice reform. The split between Black clergy that adopts a social justice platform versus those that steer clear is significant. However, there are several ways that churches can become influencers in their communities. According to Ayers and Williams (2013), the following strategies are ways to engage and not be completely submerged into a sometimes–hostile political climate: (a) letter campaigns, (b) build relationships (people power), and (c) mass meetings and rallies.

Sacrifice will be required to reach the goal of social justice. If the church is to remain the center and lead the black community the following information should be considered:

It was the destiny of the Black preachers and their churches to rise or fall with the masses. Those masses were hurting and were determined to bring an end to their misery by whatever means possible. They demanded the imposition of power—coercive power—economic, political, raw physical power, and there was justification enough in theological and ethical considerations for the Black church to follow them. Perhaps in following it would once again earn the right to lead.[33]

This statement speaks to the credibility lost as many Black Churches backed away from tackling social justice issues outside the church's four walls. The fight against injustice comes with a high price, and sacrifices must be made if future generations are to thrive in this nation.

Literature Review

One of the challenges with defining social justice is a lack of consensus on what it means. A review of social justice literature confirms various definitions categorized by academia, biblical scholars, politics, and the church. It should be no surprise that the large preponderance of literature defining social justice comes from the occupational fields of education, psychology, and social work. Social justice is globally recognized as a guiding principle in social work professional doc-

---

[33] Gayraud S. Wilmore and James H. Cone, *Black Theology* (Mary Knoll Orbis Books, 1979).

trines. However, there is a lack of clarity concerning the role of social justice within social work professional circles. "Conceptualizations of social justice among scholars, educators, and students vary greatly."[34] Social justice is a concept cited to support various actions. There is no universally agreed–upon definition. Social justice is often leveraged to support a broad spectrum of socio–political goals while focusing on just relations between groups within society.[35] Berger echoed these thoughts, emphasizing "social justice almost always has an economic, as well as policy component."[36] It was also stated "if liberals and conservatives, religious fundamentalists and radical secularists all regard their causes as socially just, how can we develop a common meaning?"[37] Other researchers stated, "social justice comes up frequently in circles concerned with political and economic policy". Bankston recognized that while ill–defined, social justice depended on two principles: (a) redistribution of

---

[34] Kimberly D. Hudson, "With Equality and Opportunity for All? Emerging Scholars Define Social Justice for Social Work: Table 1," *British Journal of Social Work* (2017), doi: 10.1093/bjsw/bcw128.

[35] J Chappelow, "Social Injustice ," https://www.investopediaco.aspm/terms/s/social-justice.asp.

[36] R.M. Berger, "What the Heck Is 'Social Justice'? *Sojourners* (2007): 37.

[37] Michael Reisch, "Defining Social Justice in a Socially Unjust World," *Families in Society: The Journal of Contemporary Social Services* 83, no. 4 (2002): 343-354, doi: 10.1606/1044-3894.17.

goods and resources and (b) the disadvantaged right to make claims on society.[38] The researcher Berger agreed, stating, "the goal of social justice is furthering the common good." From a Christian point of view, it was stated that "social charity addresses the effects of social sin, while social justice addresses the causes of such sin."[39]

This literature review examines the historical roots of social justice. It is evident that the numerous definitions for social justice fly in the face of how God defines justice. When determining a church's role in anything, there must be a clear definition for distributive and restorative justice, settling on a description that speaks to the Black Church's responsibility to champion social justice reform. The review compares what is known as "social justice" in American culture with biblical justice, principles, and actions. The review defines the Black church and its historical role in fighting injustice. It gives context to what the Black church is or is not doing to address social injustice in America.

---

[38] C. L. Bankston, "Social Justice: Cultural Origins of a Perspective Theory," *The Independent Review* 15, no. 2 (2010): 165-178.

[39] R.M. Berger, "What the Heck Is 'Social Justice'? *Sojourners* (2007): 37.

Social Justice versus Biblical Justice

Words mean something, and defining social justice can be a bit of an exercise in itself. When we do not work from the same definition and phrases, we find that, no matter how well–intentioned, we can be lead astray and into an abyss of confusion. The concept of social justice is not just a national phenomenon but a global one. The United Nations facilitated an open and informal debate with representatives from United Nations Member States and non–governmental organizations on global inequalities from the "perspective of distributive justice."[40] The United Nations Charter, Universal Declaration of Human Rights, and the International Covenants on Human Rights detail "three critical domains of equality and equity: equality of rights, equality of opportunity and equity in living conditions for all individuals and households" (p. 15). An examination of social justice literature shows that the Black church engages in social justice reform but has been inconsistent in its activism throughout the years.

Social justice is hard to define. Social justice definitions include descriptions utilizing consistent terminologies such as equality, equity, individual

---

[40] "United Nations | Peace, Dignity and Equality on a Healthy Planet," https://www.un.org/en/

freedom, civil liberties or rights, fairness, and inclusiveness are most desirable. Scholars recognize that these terms may, at times, lead to "contradictory definitions." Most scholars acknowledge that Rawls in 1971 penned the dominant formal theory of social justice.[41] Rawls defined justice as "fairness; for him, justice should rely on conditions and procedures that everyone regards as fair."[42] He identified two principles that help establish social justice. First, each person should have equal rights as all have the same rights. Secondly, those rights should be arranged to everyone's advantage. The researcher Bankston stated that social justice is distributive justice.[43] Wakefield quoted Rawls (1971) that a distributive society will "ensure every individual has access to the minimally acceptable level of economic, social, and psychological goods."[44] The United Nations concluded that social justice is synonymous with distributive justice.[45] "Social justice is the view that everyone de-

---

[41] C. L. Bankston, "Social Justice: Cultural Origins of a Perspective Theory," *The Independent Review* 15, no. 2 (2010): 165-178.

[42] F. Dionigi and J. Kleidosty, "An Analysis of John Rawls's A Theory of Justice," *Macat International* (2017).

[43] C. L. Bankston, "Social Justice: Cultural Origins of a Perspective Theory," *The Independent Review* 15, no. 2 (2010): 165-178.

[44] Jerome C. Wakefield, "Psychotherapy, Distributive Justice, and Social Work Revisited," *Smith College Studies in Social Work* 69, no. 1 (1998): 25-57, doi: 10.1080/00377319809517542.

[45] J. Baudot, "The International Forum for Social Development (Economic and Social Affairs)," *Social Justice in an Open*

serves equal economic, political, and social rights and opportunities."[46]

"Social justice means different things to different people."[47] Ornstein identified 30 basic principles considered as a framework for defining social justice. Ornstein disclosed that the following is the most significant:

Social justice is a movement for improving the lives of people, social justice depends on who interprets it and who writes the laws of society, a fair and just society will encourage equality, opportunity, and mobility, all lives matter and have equal value, a just society puts people first, bias and discrimination are minimal, individual rights supersede group rights, differences do not lead to institutional racism, laws that discriminate must be challenged. (pp. 546–548)

Ultimately, everyone bears the responsibility to call out injustice, and the government assumes the responsibility to address it. Merrett started with the definition of social justice coined by the British Commission on Social Justice, which details a hierarchy of four ideas of the Declaration of Independence: (a) the equal worth of all citizens; (b) entitlement to meet

---

World (2006): 1-146.

[46] C. L. Bankston, "Social Justice: Cultural Origins of a Perspective Theory," *The Independent Review* 15, no. 2 (2010): 165-178.

[47] Ornstein, *Social Justice, History, Purpose and Meaning*, 546-548

basic needs, self–respect and equal citizenship; (c) afforded opportunities for life chances, and (d) unjust inequalities reduced and, if possible, eliminated.[48] Chappelow supported stated "different types of social justice initiatives may exist to promote equality or redistribute power and status between groups in the areas of wealth, health, well–being, justice, privileges, and economic status."[49]

Berger stated, "justice is a moral code that guides a fair and equitable society."[50] Pipkin said, "social justice gives first place to the ethical claim of individuals and groups for conditions which make living the good life possible."[51] Reisch detailed contemporary views of social justice. Postmodern ideas link social justice with the goals of social diversity or multiculturalism. Others defined social justice in terms of empowerment. Some social work scholars defined social justice by connecting it to the struggle for gender and racial equality. Some have defined social justice concepts by aligning them with civil rights,

---

[48] Christopher D. Merrett, "Social Justice: What Is It? Why Teach It?," *Journal of Geography* 103, no. 3 (2004): 93-101, doi: 10.1080/00221340408978584.

[49] J. Chappelow, "Social Injustice ," https://www.investopediaco. aspm/terms/s/social-justice.asp.

[50] R.M. Berger, "What the Heck Is 'Social Justice'? *Sojourners* (2007): 37.

[51] C. W. Pipkin, "The Ideal of Social Justice. ," *The Southwestern Political and Social Science Quarterly* (1925): 201-202.

affirmative action, and sexual harassment language. Still, other scholars link social justice to the principle of social responsibility, opposition to oppression and domination, the eradication of racism, and poverty.[52]

It is evident by the numerous ties and tangential links that defining social justice continues to be a struggle well into the 21st century. However, several elements are common across most, if not all, the definitions previously discussed. These commonalities include, 'an ideal condition in which all members of society have the same basic rights, protection, opportunities, obligations, and social benefits."[53]

Biblical Justice

To address injustice through the body of Christ, we must examine injustice from God's view. The Bible defines for all times, and all people, what words such as truth, love, justice, and equality actually mean. These true, biblical definitions give rise to distinctively Christian cultures What can be quickly determined is that biblical justice is not commensurate with social justice. This may explain why the Black church is

---

[52] Michael Reisch, "Defining Social Justice in a Socially Unjust World," *Families in Society: The Journal of Contemporary Social Services* 83, no. 4 (2002): 343-354, doi: 10.1606/1044-3894.17.

[53] Robert L. Barker, *The Social Work Dictionary* (N A S W Press, 2003).

not "all in" with the current activist agenda. Lindsay and Nayna characterized social and biblical justice as follows, "according to the biblical worldview, people "are children of God, fashioned in His divine image. [According to] social justice, we are children of society, fashioned by its social constructions and the power dynamics they maintain."[54]

Reverend Gary Gordon of Sioux City, Iowa, stated, "The church has become overwhelmingly overrun with a parasitic false gospel of social justice. The very Christian faith that once gave birth to western civilization has been infiltrated and is even now collapsing under the weight of the parasite." (Harris, 2020, p. forward). I agree that our understanding and definition of social justice in today's environment do not align with biblical justice. I do not take the view that this social justice wave is crushing the church. One of the pressing questions concerning social justice activism is, where is the Black church in the fight against injustice? Several Black clergy march and stand with activist organizations like BLM. However, we do not see the current movement as theological, and Black pastors and clergy are not at the forefront. It was not born out of the Black church. So what is Biblical justice?

---

[54] Scott David Allen, *Why Social Justice Is Not Biblical Justice: An Urgent Appeal to Fellow Christians in a Time of Social Crisis* (Credo House Publishers, 2020) 9-10.

Baucham contrasted biblical justice and social justice. Social justice, by definition, is a state issue that is about the redistribution of advantages and resources to disadvantaged groups. It is not about individuals. It is about outcomes for groups. Biblical justice is a heart issue and the law of God. We must ask ourselves, what is the purpose or mission of justice as a Christian. Ultimately, we must align ourselves with the will and law of God. Social justice is not a heart issue.[55]

The Black Church

What is the Black church? Wilmer and Cone stated, there is an impressive array of literature on the Black Church, but the term is ambiguous.[56] The phrase "the Black church" presents details of racial and religious lifestyles unique to Black history.[57] Usually, it refers to that institution or group of Christian denominations "owned and operated" by people of African descent". Lincoln and Mamiya stated the use of the phrase "Black church" is a "sociological and theolog-

---

[55] Voddie Baucham, "Biblical Justice Vs. Social Justice | Voddie Baucham - YouTube," *Biblical Justice Vs Social Justice* , 2021, video, https://www.youtube.com/watch?v=i60eQZPG5XM.

[56] Gayraud S. Wilmore and James H. Cone, *Black Theology* (Mary Knoll Orbis Books, 1979).

[57] M.A. McMickle, "The Black Church in America - A Brief History. ," https://aaregistry.org/story/the-black-church-a-brief-history/.

ical shorthand reference to the pluralism of the Black Christian churches in the United States."[58] The Black church is the most significant institution in the Black community.[59] The Black church boasts 18 million Christians in the United States. As the center of the Black community, the church became the center to address social injustices. McKinney noted the changes in the messages of Black ministers by stating, "The Negro minister has given increasing attention to what has been called the "social gospel."[60] This social gospel offered encouragement and reminded the people that God will see that justice prevails. Pattillo–McCoy acknowledged the critics that depict the Black church as too "otherworldly" or too sedate in the face of widespread oppression. However, the Black church has a documented history of addressing social justice issues.[61]

The Black church's involvement in the civil rights movement began with the Montgomery boycott and Dr. King's reluctant emergence as the movement leader. The Black church became the base of operations

---

[58] E. C Lincoln and L. H. Mamiya, "The Black Church in the African American Experience," *Duke University Press* (1990): 163

[59] Andrew Billingsley, *Mighty Like a River* (Oxford University Press on Demand, 1999).

[60] The Black Church: Its Development and Present Impact.

[61] Mary Pattillo-McCoy, "Church Culture As a Strategy of Action in the Black Community," *American Sociological Review* 63, no. 6 (1998): 767-784, accessed May 22, 2023, doi: 10.2307/2657500.

for everything that touched the Black community. Movements and organizations such as the National Association for the Advancement of Colored People (NAACP) got their rise out of the Black church. Lowe and Shipp illustrate how community development partnerships between Black churches and historically Black colleges and universities rebuild poor and African American neighborhoods.[62] Reminiscent of a time when Black churches resisted racial oppression and social injustice, Black churches and HBCUs are partnering to make inroads into areas that have suffered neglect due to economic inequities. The Black church served as a place to mobilize and strategize moves related to fighting oppression.

According to Lincoln and Mamiya, seven major historic Black denominations arose comprising the "Black church": the African Methodist Episcopal (AME) Church; the African Methodist Episcopal Zion (AMEZ) Church; the Christian Methodist Episcopal (CME) Church; the National Baptist Convention, USA., Incorporated (NBC); the National Baptist Convention of America, Unincorporated (NBCA); the Progressive National Baptist Convention (PNBC); and the Church of God in Christ (COGIC). More than

---

[62] J. S. Lowe and S. C. Shipp, "Black Church and Black College Community Development Corporations: Enhancing the Public Sector Discourse. ," *The Western Journal of Black Studies* 38, no. 4 (2014): 244-259.

80% of all Black Christians are in these seven denominations.[63]

Given the tension in the country today, the question remains, does the Black church have a responsibility to lead or facilitate a conversation on social justice? Of course, they do. Many continue to believe that the Black church is the stalwart in the Black community. However, rising new social movements like Dream Defenders, BLM, and the Black Youth Project 100 question whether the Black church is the epicenter for social change within the Black community? To present a united front against injustice, the Black church must facilitate the conversation with potential partners in and around the community, such as HBCUs, White churches, emerging social movements, and government officials and entities.

As American culture seems to be on a collision course with itself, how does the Black church lead in reconciling a nation's differences, avoiding an unmanageable explosion of hate and anger? As the head of the church, Jesus led with His character. Christ demonstrated how to live a life of caring and love in light of tumultuous times. There are areas where the Black church can facilitate the reconciliation and restoration of century–old differences – starting with itself.

---

[63] E. C Lincoln and L. H. Mamiya, "The Black Church in the African American Experience," *Duke University Press* (1990): 163

The purpose of this literature review was to identify articles and information pertinent to defining social justice to assist the Black church in developing a strategy to address the most recent social injustices across the nation. An examination of the literature revealed a number of definitions depending on the perspective of the one doing the work. There is no consensus on the meaning of social justice; however, the consistent use of keywords such as equity, equality, and fairness provide an opportunity to reduce the confusion associated with defining the term social justice.

Lastly, how does the Black church address social justice issues through a biblical lens? Dr. King reminded us that "darkness cannot drive out darkness; only light can do that. Hate cannot drive out hate; only love can do that." The Black church has been relatively quiet minus a few pastors as this current wave of hate threatens to tear the country apart. The Black church is uniquely positioned to impact the current discourse. Studies highlight the thought processes of those in the social work field. The analysis details the frequency that keywords are used to describe social justice. The data highlight that 40% of the time, the word equality or inequality defines social justice. Other keywords that scored high include oppression, race, and racism, and human rights. Defining social justice as an "ideal condition in which all members of society have the same fundamental rights, protection, opportunities, obligations, and social benefits" addresses the ability to expand or contract based on the need of the organization defining the term.[64]

The Black church is a powerful force. Admittingly, even as Christians, our human nature makes it challenging to resist striking back when injustice rears its ugly head. We want to enforce "an eye for an eye," making the offender "pay" for their sin toward us as individuals or as a race of people. However, the Bible reminds us that the battle is not ours. It is God's, and He explicitly states in Romans 12:19b, "vengeance is mine, I will repay."[65] The Black church must address injustice in a way that brings all parties to the table in the spirit of love, condemning the violence. God intends for justice to be restorative. Restorative justice (*mishpat* in Hebrew) means seeking out vulnerable people who are being taken advantage of and helping them. It means taking steps to advocate for the weak and changing social structures to prevent injustice. The Black church has a mantle to shepherd the nation through this storm. That is what Jesus expects us to do.

---

[64] Robert L. Barker, *The Social Work Dictionary* (N A S W Press, 2003).
[65] Romans 12:19b, NKJV

CULTURAL ASPECTS
OF INJUSTICE

"**A**nd what does the Lord require of you but to do justly, to love mercy, and to walk humbly with your God?"[66]

There is a level of excitement and trepidation when you receive orders to the next duty station, especially when moving to an overseas location. It means leaving one culture and immersing yourself in another. Taking the time to learn the values, morals, priorities, and standards of an unfamiliar culture is critical. However, what you bring to the table is just as important. Each of us brings a lifetime of experiences into the organizations we join. The effectiveness of that organization depends upon each member positively contributing to the environment. It is no different for a nation, a family, or a church. What type of culture are we building, or have we created in the body of Christ? Has our culture fostered an

---

[66] Micah 6:8, NKJV

environment where the life of our brother and sisters have value or have no meaning? In 1991, I watched NBC News as Rodney King was nearly beaten to death. In 2020, I watched CBS News as George Floyd was killed with a knee on his neck. What does this nation stand for? What must the world think of us? These are questions I asked myself as cities across the country began to burn. Inciteful rhetoric stirred the consciousness of the masses. What kind of monster have we created? Nothing on the screen resembled the values this nation espouses. What is one to think of the American culture today?

The fight against injustice did not start with Rodney King. His plea in 1991 for a nation to get along has fallen on deaf ears. The murder of Michael Brown, Tamir Rice, Breonna Taylor, Freddie Gray, Ahmaud Arbery, and George Floyd are recent examples of our inability to address injustices in our culture. The root of the problem is sin and our culture's willingness to profit from that sin or injustice.[67] A capitalistic culture has contributed to the injustices we experience today. As long as there is money to be made, the injustices will continue. George Floyd's death was so egregious that numerous corporate entities have

---

[67] Tyrone Grandison, "The Root Cause Sustaining Injustice," https://tyronegrandison.medium.com/the-root-cause-sustaining-injustice-d5b7ae5eee1.

made public statements and even more public do-nations against racism and injustice. Could it be that the culture of the racist business model is no longer profitable? "There is nothing new under the sun."[68] We have been here before and have not learned the lessons. It is difficult to change a culture. Can we step back from the edge? We can; the question is, do we want to?

This chapter examines injustices within a cultural context. The Bible is often used to justify inhumane treatment according to race, gender, ethnicity, and sexual orientation. Particular verses of scripture are cherry–picked and quoted out of context. It is essential to understand the cultural context in which perceived injustices occurred. God demonstrates His concern for justice by showing love and compassion for the disenfranchised, the poor, the forgotten, and the oppressed. However, humanity consistently and regularly finds ways to pervert the Word of God by manipulating, bending, and twisting it to serve whatever nefarious purposes they aspire to. With sin firmly rooted in the world, humanity's appetite for power and dominance becomes means for oppression and unjust treatment of its citizens. However, we must examine the context in which injustices come to light within a culture.

---

[68] Ecclesiastes 1:9, NKJV

Context is king; therefore, we must remove our western cultural blinders when we examine biblical injustices within the context of biblical culture. We must first define what we mean by culture. Munroe defined culture as developing a people's intellectual capacities and moral awareness through formal instruction and informal modeling.[69] Ultimately we think and act based on the environment we grow up in. Culture manifests as a set of shared attitudes, values, goals, and practices that characterize a racial, religious, or social group. Just because the culture may change does not mean the Word of God changes. Stott's words provide the perfect backdrop to understanding cultural context:

> No word of the Bible was spoken in a cultural vacuum. Every part of it was culturally conditioned. This is not to say that the local culture controlled its message in such a way as to be distorted by it, but rather that the local culture was the medium through which God expressed himself. We must be careful what deductions we draw from it. Both sides have taken extreme positions in the debate. Some will declare that whenever they find biblical teaching couched in cultural terms other than their own, the teaching is irrelevant

---

[69] Myles Munroe, *Understanding Your Place in God* (Destiny Image Publishers, 2011).

because the culture is alien. Others make the opposite mistake and invest both the kernel of the teaching and the cultural shell with equal normative authority. The more prudent way, however, is to preserve the inner substance of what God is teaching or commanding while claiming the liberty to re–clothe it in modern cultural dress. We will examine regional biases, gender, ethnicity, race, sexuality, and medical discrimination to understand how culture contributes to widespread injustice.[70]

Hostility Toward Samaria

Throughout history, hostility against people, regions, and nations often leads to conflicts and atrocities that redefine both the one perpetuating the hate and the one receiving it. The genesis of the hostility ranges from water rights, land ownership, cultural differences, and religious affiliation, to name a few. Hatred can then lead to several injustices between the hostile parties. Samaria and Israel is one such conflict.

Samaria, also known as Palestine, was founded by King Omri approximately 880 B.C. Historically, the city of Samaria was not known for keeping the Jew-

---

[70] J. Stott, "Culture and the Bible," https://ism.intervarsity.org/resource/culture-and-bible.

ish statutes. King Ahab build a temple for the pagan god, Baal, in the city. The town was under siege by Shalmaneser V, king of Assyria, and then Sargon II, who destroyed the city and exiled the citizens to Assyria. After the Assyrian conquest in 722 B.C.

Assyria resettled the area with foreigners who brought their pagan gods and customs. The resettlement perpetuated the intermarriage of Israelites with foreigners, a violation of Deuteronomy 7:3–5.[71] The scripture forbids the intermarrying of Israelites and foreigners, stating, "they will turn your sons away from following Me, to serve other gods; so the anger of the Lord will be aroused against you and destroy you suddenly.[72] The Jews accused the Samaritans of idolatry, leaving their faith, and considered them a mongrel race. Samaritans were considered "dogs" or "half–breeds." The breaking of the Mosaic law, coupled with the fact that the Samaritans were, in part, a remnant of some of the 10 tribes of the Northern Kingdom, which had earlier separated themselves from the kingdom of Judah, could explain the dislike most Jews displayed for the Samaritans.

When the Jews started to build the Temple in Jerusalem, the Samaritans offered to help but were

---

[71] Deuteronomy 7:3–5, NKJV
[72] Deuteronomy 7:4, NKJV

refused and considered unfit to do so.[73] Hostilities intensified when the Samaritans built their own temple on Mount Gerizim in 332 B.C., proclaiming it as God's holy place. This was considered an act of blasphemy by the Jews. Cole posited the temple on Mount Gerizim resulted from Samaritans' inability to worship freely in Jerusalem due to prejudice.[74] The Jews burned it around 128 B.C., intensifying the relationship between the Jews and the Samaritans. Samaria deepened the hostility by claiming only the Pentateuch (Genesis–Deuteronomy) is God's law, rejecting all the books of poetry and prophecy.

The hostility against Samaritans continued well into the first century. Devout Jews would go many miles out of their way to avoid traveling through the region. Yet, in John 4, we see Jesus making an intentional stop in Samaria where he meets the woman at the well. She is surprised that Jesus speaks to her as Jews did not interact with the Samaritans, especially women of questionable character. Jesus asks her for a drink. During this period in history, it was unusual for a Jewish person to ask a favor or accept a drink from a Samaritan's cup. The disciples were also surprised that Jesus spoke to her. Rabbis were forbid-

---

[73] Ezra 4:1–3

[74] L.G. Cole, "The Samaritans: A Yesterday People Today.," https://churchofjesuschrist.org.

den to greet a woman in public. In verses 16–19, Jesus asks the woman to get her husband. His request is culturally appropriate even though He knows she has no husband.[75]

The question of worship is addressed as the woman distinguishes Mount Gerizim from Jerusalem for worship. Jesus tells her "you worship what you do not know." Jesus makes a sharp contrast between the Jews and the Samaritans, associating himself with the Jews.[76] His comment about neither worshiping on the mountain or in Jerusalem is a pivot to the spiritual relationship and covenant one makes with Christ. Is this not what the church is all about? The process of leading people to accept the living water of Christ. Regardless of their cultural affiliations.

Gender Discrimination

Women in ancient Israel participated in every aspect of community life to include commerce and real estate.[77] Manual labor was exhibited by Ruth in gleaning the fields.[78] Women were not excluded from worshiping, praying, and participating in ceremonies at the

---

[75] D. Guzik, "John 4 - A Samaritan Woman and a Nobleman Meet Jesus," https://enduringword.com/bible-commentary/john-4/.

[76] Ibid

[77] Proverbs 31, NKJV

[78] Ruth 2:7, NKJV

Temple. The only area women could not participate in was the Temple priesthood. God required women to be present at the reading of the scriptures.[79] But by the first century, the role of women drastically changed.

In the first century, the concept of tzenuah (modesty) based on Psalm 45:13, "All glorious is the princess in her chamber," glorified the private role of women and elevated the more public role of men.[80] Influenced by the Greco–Roman culture, the treatment of women took on new meaning. This culture places tremendous importance on order and classification; there was a "place for everyone and everyone in his place." A person's "place" was pre–determined by age, gender, level of freedom (slave, freed, and freeborn), and citizenship and required a particular behavior in keeping with one's position.[81] The rights of women begin to diminish with the rise of the Roman Empire. There was no co–mingling of men and women in the Temple. Women could visit the Temple but not move beyond the Women's Court.

Why are women nearly excluded from society during the first century? The "degraded" view of

---

[79] Deuteronomy 31:12

[80] Psalm 45:13, NKJV

[81] D.P. Delong, *Woman and Culture in the New Testament World* (Leaven, 2012).

women originated with the Greek.[82] The similarities between the Hellenistic and Talmudic opinions of women are remarkable. The Greeks influenced the rabbis' previous acceptance of women, slowly relegating them to seclusion. Women were to support the education and training of men. They were not to embarrass the family or brin dishonor or shame.

Many nameless women in the scriptures are identified by the man they married (Lot's wife, Job's wife, and Peter's wife). There are no names provided for Jesus' sisters, Jarius' daughter, or Paul's sister either.[83] The consensus is that unnamed characters in biblical texts are not important and therefore not given prominent attention, thus ignoring or downplaying them.[84] The Hebrew Bible and culture are male–oriented in authorship, subject matter, and perspectives.[85] According to Trible, anonymity is not only a symbol of unimportance but also denotes a

---

[82] Z. Glaser, "The Role of Women in the Bible ," https://jewsforjesus.org/publications/newsletter/newsletter-jun-1988/the-role-of-women-in-the-bible/

[83] Lockyer, "Chapter 3. Nameless Bible Women - Lockyer," accessed May 23, 2023, https://www.biblegateway.com/resources/all-women-bible/Chapter-3-Nameless-Bible-Women.

[84] David T. Adamo, "A Silent Unheard Voice in the Old Testament: The Cushite Woman Whom Moses Married in Numbers 12:1–10," *In die Skriflig/In Luce Verbi* 52, no. 1 (2018): 1-8, doi: 10.4102/ids.v52i1.2370.

[85] Jennie R. Ebeling, *Women* (A&C Black, 2010).

"lack of power and personhood."[86] Brenner stated, "the absence of proper name not only erases narrative identity but symbolizes the suppression of women in Israelite society."[87]

We see this marginalization of women when Jesus confronts the "women at the well." John 4:27 describes the astonishment of the disciples as Jesus "talked with a woman; yet no one said, "What do You seek?" or, "Why are You talking with her?" Speaking in public for women was criticized and considered inappropriate behavior. A woman must guard her speech in public. Learning and debating were masculine traits and undesirable for women. Women who violated the "law" were subject to divorce without compensation.[88]

The differences in the roles and allowances made for women in ancient Israel and the first century can be traced back to Greco–Roman cultural influences in the first century. First–century society did not welcome women into the public sphere. It further marginalized those who dared to step outside it. Yet, the

---

[86] Phyllis Trible, *Texts of Terror* (Fortress Press, 1984).

[87] Athalya Brenner, *A Feminist Companion to Judges* (Sheffield Press, 1993).

[88] Z. Glaser, "The Role of Women in the Bible ," https://jewsforjesus.org/publications/newsletter/newsletter-jun-1988/the-role-of-women-in-the-bible/

Bible is full of women who accomplished much for the kingdom.

The Syrophoenician Woman - Gender and Ethnicity (Mark 7:24-30)

Jesus' treatment of the Syrophoenician woman could be interpreted as prejudicial and rude. She is triply marginalized in this culture as a woman, Gentile, and foreigner (Setzer, 2019). Jesus traveled with the disciples to Tyre and Sidon region, which is considered present–day Syria, Lebanon, Turkey, and Israel. Jesus' travel outside Jewish territory could be seen as an eventual expansion of his ministry. Jesus was withdrawing from conflict with the Pharisees and elders of the Temple. He enters Gentile territory where the Canaanites reside. They are bitter enemies of the Israelites and are a pagan society. Mark tells the story of an unnamed woman who follows Jesus down the street and yells to him, asking that he heal her daughter. There is a recognition of his sovereignty as she calls him Son of David. Jesus does not acknowledge the woman as if to see if she would continue her plea.

The disciples are annoyed that a woman dares to even speak to Jesus as women are forbidden in this culture to speak in public. The woman falls at Jesus' feet and repeats her request. Some would say that Jesus' response was harsh as He replies, "Let the children be filled first, for it is not good to take the children's bread and throw it to the little dogs." The children refer to the children of Israel. Dogs have a negative connotation and mean impure, outsiders, non–Jews. The woman's response is bold. She has nothing to lose and is pleading for her child. She argues, "Yes, Lord, yet even the little dogs under the table eat from the children's crumbs."[89] Jesus is pleased with her response, praising her and subsequently heals her daughter. Jesus emphasizes in this exchange the priority the children of Israel have over everyone else, even if they will not receive him. The Jew rejected him, but a Gentile woman stepped out on faith and sought him.

Racial Injustice - The Case for Interracial Marriage (Numbers 12)

During the height of Jim Crowism, interracial relationships did not garner favor, particularly in the South. They were met with hostility and, many times, death. Black men could not speak to White women, and White men were rebuked for dating or marrying a Black woman. We read in the 12th chapter of Numbers that Moses experienced the same scrutiny for his marriage to a dark–skinned woman. Chapter 12

---

[89] Mark 7:28, NKJV

begins with Miriam and Aaron attacking Moses for his choice of women. Verse one states, "then Miriam and Aaron spoke against Moses because of the Ethiopian woman whom he had married; for he had married an Ethiopian woman." A couple of things strike me about this family dispute. First, the Bible does not tell us if Moses had another wife other than Zipporah, who was of Midianite descent. Still, Miriam emphasized "Ethiopian in the KJV," the NIV says, "Cushite," a term used in the Hebrew Bible to refer to Africa and Africans. Ancient Egyptians seem to refer to Black Africans in their southern border as 'Kushu or Kush.[90] Secondly, as a Hebrew, Miriam had dark skin as well. It was not as dark as Moses' wife, but it was not White. Miriam used the term to be hurtful. There are two beliefs as to why Miriam and Aaron had a problem with the Cushite woman. First, the Torah's Aramaic translation suggests Miriam and Aaron were angry about a separation. The interpretation points to Exodus 18:2, where Jethro brings Moses his wife. Given women's status in this society, divorce or separation would negatively affect Moses' wife.[91] Some rabbinic scholars believed Miriam and Aaron's concern centered on

---

[90] David T. Adamo, "A Silent Unheard Voice in the Old Testament: The Cushite Woman Whom Moses Married in Numbers 12:1–10," *In die Skriflig/In Luce Verbi* 52, no. 1 (2018): 1-8, accessed May 23, 2023, doi: 10.4102/ids.v52i1.2370
[91] Exodus 18:2, NKJV

the possibility that Moses married a non–Israelite. Regardless of why, the bigger question is, why did Miriam think it was permissible to speak against Moses' in this manner?

Racial prejudice and jealousy take center stage in this exchange between Miriam, Aaron, and Moses. Miriam and Aaron may have felt Moses should consult them in all matters. Ultimately the attack is about Moses' authority. While Moses was not bothered by Miriam's petty behavior, God was not pleased. In verse 10, "suddenly Miriam became leprous, as White *as* snow. Then Aaron turned toward Miriam, and there she was, a leper." God's instant "justice" revealed Miriam's, selfish heart. Protecting his own interest, Aaron quickly repented confessing their foolish behavior against Moses. Moses had not spoken in his own defense yet intercedes for Miriam's healing. God does heal her, but she must remain outside the camp for seven days.[92] Miriam was an example of the price paid for selfish ambition, attempting to disparage God's ordained.

The Ethiopian Eunuch (Acts 8:26-40)

In the original texts of the Bible, a "eunuch" is termed saris (Hebrew, Old Testament) or eunouchos (Greek,

---

[92] Number 2: 14–16

New Testament). However, both these words could, apart from meaning a castrate, also refer to an official or a commander.[93] There is a long history of eunuchs involved in the courts of Egypt, Assyria, and Persia. They protect the queen and manage the king's harem, and in many cases, eunuchs are the most trusted advisors.

The story of the Ethiopian eunuch generally focuses on the eunuch's salvation and the spread of the word to Gentile territory, specifically Africa. However, no commentary is given addressing why Phillip had to meet the eunuch in the desert in the first place. Luke tells us the eunuch had been to Jerusalem to worship. However, he could not worship due to discriminatory practices at the Temple. If the eunuch had known Deuteronomy 23:1[94] states, "He who is emasculated by crushing or mutilation shall not enter the assembly of the Lord." He may not have made the journey.

Looking at this story through the eyes of the eunuch reveals the discriminatory practices that God used to convert a Gentile and advance the kingdom. The story depicts an outsider wishing to worship in

---

[93] FP Retief, JFG Cilliers, and SPJK Riekert, "Eunuchs in the Bible," *Acta Theologica* 26, no. 2 (2010): 247-258, doi: 10.4314/actat.v26i2.52578.

[94] Deuteronomy 23:1, NKJV

the Temple and is denied the ability to do so. The scriptures do not name the eunuch. Luke describes him in Acts 8:27 as "a man of Ethiopia, a eunuch of great authority under Candace, the queen of the Ethiopians, who had charge of all her treasury."[95] He was literate, wealthy, and successful in his position, and a person of faith. He journeyed from his native land to Jerusalem. The trip would have taken weeks to complete. Imagine his disappointment at being denied entry to the Temple to fulfill the reason for the journey. Dahl emphasized that the man was a eunuch, and he should not have access to the Jewish Temple. Therefore he "represents a person at the fringe of Judaism." He is an outsider. Yet, he is hungry for the word.[96]

Acts 8 tells the story of the Ethiopian eunuch converted to Christianity by the Apostle Philip. An angel of the Lord directs Phillip to go south on a desert road leading to Jerusalem and Gaza. Philip obeys and meets the eunuch, who was returning home. A sign of his wealth, the eunuch purchased a scroll containing the Book of Isaiah.[97] Philip saw him reading Isaiah 53:7–8 that prophesied the coming Messiah

---

[95] Acts 8: 27, NKJV

[96] N. Dahl, "Nations in the New Testament. New Testament Christianity for Africa and the World: Essays in Honor of Harry Sawyer," (1973): 54-68.

[97] Acts 8, NKJV

and asked if he understood what he was reading. The eunuch responded in verse 31, "How can I, unless someone guides me?" And he asked Philip to come up and sit with him."[98]

Philip interpreted the scripture for him, and they continued traveling south together until they came upon a body of water. The eunuch asks Philip, "What hinders me from being baptized?"[99] Philip asks the eunuch if he believes that Jesus Christ is the Son of God. The eunuch expresses his belief, and Philip baptizes him. Philip is immediately taken away by the Holy Spirit to Azotus, and the eunuch went away rejoicing.

Ethiopia embraced Christianity and has maintained its doctrines from the era of the apostles to the present day. After the eunuch's conversion and subsequent return home, Irenaeus writes that he preached the Gospel to the Ethiopians. Eusebius speaks of this eunuch as the first fruits of the faith in the whole world. The eunuch's conversion marks the beginning of the Ethiopian Orthodox Church. As with so many other biblical stories, the marginalized become the heralded heroes for the kingdom.

---

[98] Isaiah, 53: 7, NKJV
[99] Acts 8:36, NKJV

Discrimination against the Disabled

The Hebrew word mum, usually translated as "blemish," refers to many conditions that we may consider a disability.[100] The word "blemish" originally meant a "black spot." It later came to denote anything abnormal or deviating from a given standard, whether physical, moral, or ritualistic. The word "blemish" was used to describe the various abnormalities that disqualify one from the priesthood.[101] Yet the Bible does not use the word mum for conditions such as deafness or muteness, even though these conditions are sometimes paired with other conditions that qualify as a mum (e.g., the pairing of 'blind' and 'deaf' in Leviticus 19:14; Isaiah 29:18; 35:5; 43:8).[102] The most common diseases mentioned in the Bible are blindness, deafness, dumbness, leprosy, and paralysis. Visual impairment is the most common form of physical disability (Otieno, 2009).

In biblical culture, disabilities were viewed as a disease, not meeting the culture's normality standards. People with disabilities were shunned for various reasons. Some conditions, such as deafness–dumbness

---

[100] Leviticus 21:16–23, NKJV

[101] Cyrus Adler and Isidore Singer, *The Jewish Encyclopedia* (1925).

[102] Jeremy Schipper, *Disability Studies and the Hebrew Bible: Figuring Mephibosheth in the David Story* (New York: T.T. Clark , 2006).

or epileptic seizures, were associated with demonic activity. Other conditions occur due to previous sin, whether committed by the disabled person or his or her ancestors. Even the Levitical law prevented disabled persons from becoming priests or conducting priestly activities. The exclusion led to assumptions that disabled people are second–class citizens.[103] According to Schipper, "the Hebrew Bible does not propose such a theology or present disability as a problem to be solved.[104]

The general view of the Old Testament writers is that God brings disability as punishment for transgressions for sin or as an expression of God's wrath for people's disobedience. It is seen as a curse and a result of unbelief and ignorance. Given this perspective, individuals with disabilities are considered unworthy in society and often view themselves unworthy as a result of the abuse they receive. In 2 Samuel 19:24–28, King David's servant, Ziba, prohibits Mephibosheth, who was physically impaired, from joining David on a trip. Ziba deemed him unfit to be in the company of King David because of his disability. Mephibosheth himself feels unworthy. In verse 26,

---

[103] G. G Scorgie, *Dictionary of Christian Spirituality* (Grand Rapids: Zondervan, 2011).Your bibliography:

[104] Jeremy Schipper, *Disability Studies and the Hebrew Bible: Figuring Mephibosheth in the David Story* (New York: T.T. Clark , 2006). 129

Mephibosheth says, "My Lord the King, since I your servant am lame."[105]

In 2 Samuel 4:4, we learn that Mephibosheth became lame when his nurse dropped him while fleeing.[106] It was customary to execute anyone connected with the previous dynasty. However, David wanted to help the family of his enemy. Mephibosheth was the son of Jonathan and the rightful heir to the throne. However, his disability excluded him from ascending to the throne.[107] Mephibosheth allows his disability to affect his self-esteem. The psychological effects of a disability weigh heavily in this story. Mephibosheth responds to David's generosity in 2 Samuel 9:8, saying, "What is your servant, that you should look upon such a dead dog as I?"[108]

Throughout the Bible, disabilities like blindness and deafness are used as metaphors for ignorance or a lack of comprehension, reflecting ancient cultural attitudes towards disability. The culture viewed disabilities as deficiencies versus differences. The reason metaphors worked in their ancient context and are still relatable in today's culture is the nega-

---

[105] Samuel 19:24–28, NKJV

[106] 2 Samuel 4:4, NKJV

[107] M. Henning, "Disabilities in the Bible - Bible Odyssey," https://www.bibleodyssey.org/people/related-articles/disabilities-in-the-bible/.

[108] 2 Samuel 9:8, NKJV

tive value placed upon bodies that are different from what is considered the norm. Henning drew a parallel between disability and sin.[109] In John 5:14, Jesus heals a paralyzed man and tells him, "See, you have been made well. Sin no more, lest a worse thing come upon you."[110] In John 9:2, the disciples meet a man who was born blind and ask Jesus, "Rabbi, who sinned, this man or his parents, that he was born blind?"[111] In both of these scriptures, the underlying assumption is that individual sin causes disability. In this context, Jesus' healings and his response to the question subtly undermine the idea that sin causes disabilities, even while the Gospel of John reinforces the cultural norm.[112]

Taken out of context, one could say that the Bible discriminates against the disabled. The scripture used to support this contention is Leviticus 21:16–23, which states,

And the Lord spoke to Moses, saying, "Speak to Aaron, saying: 'No man of your descendants

---

[109] M. Henning, "Disabilities in the Bible - Bible Odyssey," https://www.bibleodyssey.org/people/related-articles/disabilities-in-the-bible/.

[110] John 5:14, NKJV

[111] John 9: 2, NKJV

[112] M. Henning, "Disabilities in the Bible - Bible Odyssey," https://www.bibleodyssey.org/people/related-articles/disabilities-in-the-bible/.

in succeeding generations, who has any defect, may approach to offer the bread of his God. For any man who has a defect shall not approach: a man blind or lame, who has a marred face or any limb too long, a man who has a broken foot or broken hand, or is a hunchback or a dwarf, or a man who has a defect in his eye, or eczema or scab, or is a eunuch. No man of the descendants of Aaron the priest, who has a defect, shall come near to offer the offerings made by fire to the Lord. He has a defect; he shall not come near to offer the bread of his God. He may eat the bread of his God, both the most holy and the holy; only he shall not go near the veil or approach the altar, because he has a defect, lest he profane My sanctuaries; for I the Lord sanctify them. [113]

Priests came from the tribe of Levi. These restrictions were not to discriminate against the disabled but to show the purity and separation from sin required to represent the people before God. Here disabilities are used as metaphors that equate to spiritual disabilities. While those with disabilities could not join the priesthood, it did not preclude them from having a covenant relationship with God.

---

[113] Leviticus 21:16–23, NKJV

God uses disabilities to demonstrate His grace. We are created in God's image, the disabled and the able-bodied. Moses had a speech impediment, yet it did not stop him from being used by God. Paul was blinded on the road to Damascus when he met Christ. We know from Paul's writings in Galatians 4:13–14 that he suffered with eye problems.[114] Paul recognizes that he was well-received despite his disability, stating, "You know that because of physical infirmity I preached the gospel to you at the first. And my trial which was in my flesh you did not despise or reject, but you received me as an angel of God, even as Christ Jesus."[115] Elijah carried great spiritual authority, rained fire from heaven, and fearless in challenging the king. Still, he suffered from depression and suicidal ideation. Many are stigmatized in their fight against mental illness.

The lessons for the church are clear. God will use whomever He chooses to accomplish His plan and purpose. When it comes to disabilities, Waggoner asked, "Who is more disabled: the person with special needs or the pastor and congregation which are unable to cope with their needs."[116] Is the church

---

[114] R. Bayes, "A Biblical View of Disability," https://www.bethinking. org/human-life/a-biblical-view-of-disability.

[115] Galatians 4:13-14, NKJV

[116] S. Waggoner, "Normal Is Not Biblical: An Explaratory Study of Ministry With Developmental Diabilities in the Arkansas

minimizing someone's ability or worth because of a disability, or are we able to see that everyone has a purpose? We need to seek God for it.

Many people with mental illness will never seek help because our culture has stigmatized the issue. The perceived shame associated with mental illness keeps those that need help hidden and on the margins of society. We have done a better job in trying to erase the stigma but we have a long way to go. The cultural backdrop will have to continue to change dramatically to make a significant difference in this area. The church can play an active role in identifying those who may need help within their congregations. It starts with communication and showing love, just as Jesus would do.

As I approach my birthday, I realize that my eyes are growing dimmer, my limbs are a bit stiffer, and I move a whole lot slower these days. We all will face disability in some way as we age. God has a purpose for each of us. Disabilities offer God a way to demonstrate His healing, restoration, and grace as we accomplish what He called us to do.

Conference of the United Methodist Church," (2017).

Key Takeaways

- Culture is one of the most talked-about topics in today's corporate environment. It continues to be one of the most pressing concerns for executives. But what about the church? Are we as concerned about the culture in the church environment as we are with our work environment? We observed the oppressive nature of biblical culture in each of the stories mentioned above. Younger generations expect a loving, vibrant, and nurturing environment. They expect the church to consistently stand on biblical principles in developing a climate where all are welcome to worship. They expect to be consistently engaged and presented opportunities that will challenge them to work in the kingdom. The older crowd has expectations as well. They prefer a bit of tradition. Balancing the traditional with technology can be a challenge, but one worth exploring to ensure everyone matures in Christ.

- Faith does not always come in the package we expect. Jesus' conversation with the Syrophoenician woman demonstrated that those that do not necessarily believe as you do are still worthy of compassion and love. How many times have we judged a person by their cultural background, gender, race, sex, or how they dress and assume that they cannot understand the finer points of life as we see them. The woman came from a pagan background yet believed Jesus would heal her daughter.

- We all must be aware of our cultural blinders. How we see the world and each other feeds the negativity we continue to see today. Our experiences, good or bad, lay the foundation for how we will ultimately treat others.

- The Black Church is influential within the community. The church must leverage its influence to engage social and political entities to push for positive change.

It is one thing to say there is a need for change and quite another to implement that change. Take a moment to evaluate your church's culture and discuss it with your ministerial team.

Questions for Reflection and Discussion

Evaluate your church culture. There are several tools to use in evaluating your culture. One such tool is the Assessment of Church Culture by Cameron and Quinn (1999). It can be found at https://cdn.bgco.org/2011/10/01122129/Church-Culture-Assessment.pdf

Below are questions that can help facilitate a discussion on church culture.

1. Are there areas where your ministry team can improve? If so, what are they?

____

____

2. Identify your cultural blinders. Are you interacting with people or the community based on how you see them through your cultural lens, or are you seeing them through God's eyes?

____

____

3. How can your church use its influence to effect positive social change?

____

____

4. Does your church culture exclude others?

____

____

____

JUSTICE SERVED - BIBLICALLY

ar be it from You to do such a thing as this, to slay the righteous with the wicked, so that the righteous should be as the wicked; far be it from You! Shall not the Judge of all the earth do right?"[117]

Suffice it to say that I was not the most obedient child and received my share of whippings. I was bully at times, and I am sure I had a whole lot more coming to me, but there were times I felt actions toward me were unfair. Even in our youth, we have an idea of what we think justice is, especially if wrongly accused or punished. Parents believe they are quoting scripture by saying, "spare the rod, spoil the child," as they administer the licks. This saying is not biblical! To set the record straight, Proverbs 13:24 states, "He who spares his rod hates his son, but he who loves him disciplines him promptly."[118] We see God's discipline in His interactions with His people throughout scripture. It is easy to assume that God

117 Genesis 18:25, NKJV
118 Proverbs 13:24

exacted justice on the Israelites for their disobedience given biblical stories and history. I want to assure you that not all the troubles experienced in our world result from disobedience and judgment. However, the Old Testament reminds us that many of the issues the nation of Israel endured were a direct result of God's judgment.

The Bible is a detailed history of humanity's disobedience and rebellion against God and how He dealt and currently deals with that disobedience through love and punishment. Imagine if your parents were so angry with you that their final recourse was to wipe you off the face of the earth. The great flood is a great example of how God unleashed His brand of justice on the earth. Genesis 6 tells us God was not going to allow mankind to continue in rebellion against Him. In verse 3, God speaks, "My Spirit shall not strive with man forever, for he is indeed flesh; yet his days shall be one hundred and twenty years."[119] God gave humanity an opportunity to turn the corner on their disobedience. It took 120 years for him to prepare Noah for his purpose to prepare the ark. In his infinite mercy, I believe He wanted to see humanity change their behavior and return to Him. Genesis 6:6 depicts God's heart toward man, stating, "and the LORD was sorry that He had made man on

---

[119] Genesis 6: 3, NKJV

the earth, and He was grieved in His heart."[120] But make no mistake, God is not soft on sin. The flood was a do–over, an opportunity for humanity to start again—Noah and his family were the witnesses of His justice in humanity's disobedience.

Joseph is another instance where you read the story and say to yourself; there is no justice in anything that happened to Joseph. His brothers conspire to kill him but instead sell him into slavery. Potiphar's wife accuses him of rape and is thrown in prison. However, God issued justice in Joseph's life, albeit 23 years later, before Joseph became governor of Egypt and fulfilled his purpose for the children of Israel. Jesus made us think about justice by making us examine ourselves in John 8:5–7. The scribes and Pharisees brought a woman caught in adultery to be judged by Jesus. The accusation was made public to embarrass the woman and trap Jesus in the execution of Mosaic Law. If Jesus allows her to be set free, He is viewed as breaking the laws of Moses.[121] If Jesus follows the law and has her stoned, He is seen as harsh. Instead of passing judgment on the woman, Jesus judged those that brought her before him, asking why the one who witnessed the act was not before him as well. His statement in verse 10 to the woman, "go

---

[120] Genesis 6:6, NKJV
[121] John 8:5–7, NKJV

and sin no more," was a reinforcement of not passing judgment on the woman. Unfortunately, we have a desire to point out and punish the sins of others while ignoring our own sin. This was the case with King David when Nathan the Prophet told him the story of a man who stole and killed another man's pet lamb.[122] King David was angry and condemned the man to death. He was not looking at the man in the mirror, his own sin with Bathsheba.

These are just a few examples of many that demonstrate how God adjudicates His law with His people. But why does God even care? He already knows how the story ends. He allowed humanity to make choices, so why is justice so important anyway? If we mess it up, we have to live with it – right? Let's look at what scripture says. Psalm 89:14 states, "Righteousness and justice *are* the foundation of Your throne; Mercy and truth go before Your face."[123] God included justice in the foundation of His creation. It is in our DNA to pursue justice in unjust situations. Injustice is rooted in sin; God hates sin. Sin is a crime against God, and justice demands a penalty of death and separation from Him. Justice and righteousness are a part of God's character and originates from His Holiness. However, God's mercy and grace, many

---

122 2 Samuel 12:1–10, NKJV
123 Psalm 89:14, NKJV

times, temper His anger toward his children. To ensure we in the new covenant can be reconciled back to Him, God sent Jesus.

This chapter will investigate several injustices perpetrated against God's chosen people and how He resolved them. From the Old Testament, we will examine Egypt's oppression of the Hebrews in slavery through Moses' interaction with Pharoah and a request to "let my people go", King David's adjudication of justice for sins against the Gibeonites, and Haman's attempt at genocide in the Book of Esther. We will examine New Testament injustices through the lens of Saul and his persecution of the church. Finally, we will review the Book of Revelation and God's final Judgement of humanity. We will also examine how Dr. Martin Luther King Jr. looked to scripture in developing a nonviolence policy to fight against racial injustice. The Civil Rights Movement eventually resulted in a change in legislation to address racial injustices across the country.

According to Baucham, biblical justice is a heart issue, and the law of God.[124] Allen presented biblical justice as "conformity to God's moral standard as revealed in the Ten Commandments and the Royal

---

[124] Voddie Baucham, "Biblical Justice Vs. Social Justice | Voddie Baucham - YouTube," *Biblical Justice Vs Social Justice* , 2021, video, https://www.youtube.com/watch?v=i60eQZPG5XM.

Law: "love your neighbor as yourself."[125] Metzger (2010) stated, "The theology of justice flows from the heart of God" (p. 1). Beisner discusses the four criteria for justice, key concepts detailed in the Bible.[126] First, when Moses commissioned Israel's judges. He charged them to:

> Hear the cases [shaphat, "judge"] between your brethren, and judge [shaphat] righteously [tsedeq] between a man and his brother or the stranger who is with him. You shall not show partiality in judgment [mishpat]; you shall hear the small as well as the great; you shall not be afraid in any man's presence, for the judgment [mishpat] is God's."[127]

Secondly, in Romans 13:7, Paul directed believers to "render to all their due." God is the chief judge rendering to each man according to his deeds.[128] Therefore, a key concept is "something about the person being judged merits the judgment."[129] The third criteria require justice to be proportional. Meaning is

---

125 Scott David Allen, *Why Social Justice Is Not Biblical Justice: An Urgent Appeal to Fellow Christians in a Time of Social Crisis* (Credo House Publishers, 2020).

126 E. Calvin Beisner, *Social Justice* (Family Research Council, 2013).

127 Deuteronomy 1:16–17, NKJV

128 Proverbs 24:12, NKJV

129 E. Calvin Beisner, *Social Justice* (Family Research Council, 2013).

the reward or punishment commensurate to the act? This involves an investigation of whether the injustice was intentional or accidental. Or was the harm done against a person or property.[130] The fourth criterion requires "conformity to the standard set in God's law, including the Ten Commandments, moral statutes, and ordinances."[131] Now that we have a better understanding of biblical justice and its criteria. Let's investigate how God brings justice to the kingdom.

Justice for the Oppressed

Oppression is the unjust use of power at other people's expense. Kranz stated, "It involves protecting one's power, comfort, security, and privilege at the expense of those with less of these than you."[132] The Israelites have a history of oppression and slavery, enduring 400 years of oppression and slavery under Egyptian rule. Written by Moses, the Book of Exodus details the victories and failures of a people God chose as his own. Freed from captivity to establish a new life in the promised land, Exodus demonstrates God's judgment and mercy as He guided the Israel-

---

[130] Leviticus 24: 17–21, NKJV

[131] Leviticus 19:35–36, NKJV

[132] "Oppression and Social Justice in the Bible: A Beginner's Guide," *Beginner's Guide to the Bible* (2020).

ites through the wilderness to the land of milk and honey.

A new Pharoah saw the Israelites as a threat to his kingdom as they grew in number and strength and were mightier than the Egyptians.[133] The Hebrew were building Pithom and Raamses and were used to hard labor, making them strong people. On the advice of counsel, Pharoah oppressed the Hebrews but the more he oppressed them, the more they multiplied and grew.[134] Pharoah, in his paranoia, felt his security was threatened and enslaved the Hebrews and ordered that the male children be killed. In the first chapter of Exodus, we see the seeds of hate for a people that had not been a threat to Egyptian governance become a tree of injustice.

God does not deal with this injustice right away. He is preparing Moses for the leadership role he will assume. We notice that time is not a factor for God. It took a total of 80 years before Moses was ready to approach Pharoah. God, having heard his people's cry's for deliverance, Moses received his direction, and Aaron assumed the position as Moses' assistant. Moses and Aaron meet with Pharoah, requesting that he allow the Hebrews a three–day pilgrimage to go into the wilderness and offer sacrifices to God.

---

[133] Exodus 1:9, NKJV
[134] Exodus 1:12, NKJV

Pharoah denied the request and hardened the labor on the Hebrews. With each denial, Pharoah's heart hardened all the more. Pharaoh's refusal to let the Hebrews go resulted in 10 plagues. After each denial, Pharoah would reap the consequences of his hardened heart. Justice for the Hebrews came in a series of plagues. Each plague gets progressively worse as God ushers Pharoah through each phase on several occasions, providing a warning before each plague arrives. According to Guzik, "the plagues God brought against Egypt had a definite strategy and purpose. Each of them confronts and attacks a prized Egyptian deity."[135]

The consequences of denying freedom to the Hebrews cost the Egyptians everything, ultimately the firstborn child. Pharoah finally allowed the Hebrews to depart Egypt but was soon overcome with rage and chased the Hebrews to the banks of the Red Sea. The final act of justice toward Pharoah was the destruction of his army getting swallowed by the Red Sea after the Hebrews crossed on dry land. The freeing of the Hebrews illustrated how God dealt with the injustices Pharoah directed toward the Hebrews. It is important to note that God hardened Pharoah's heart. It was a simple matter of giving Pharoah over

---

[135] D. Guzik, "Exodus 7- Miracles and Plagues Before Pharoah," *Enduring Word* (2020).

to his own sin. Pharoah was warned, yet he made the decisions that brought destruction.

The Exodus story is ripe with injustices. There are numerous times the Hebrews found themselves on the negative side of God's judgment. What should have been a two-week trip to the promised land took 40 years. They lost the vision that God set before them and literally lost their way both spiritually and physically. Maxwell said of the Hebrews, "God's people failed to cooperate, doubted the vision, disobeyed the rules, worshiped material things, forgot their goals and soured on their leader – delaying their dream forty years."[136] However, what was designed by the enemy to shame the Hebrew nation, killing of the first born, ultimately saved them. God's formula for Justice never looks like we think it should. Not only were the people freed but they left with riches from the Egyptians. If we, God's people, obey and walk in righteousness, there is nothing He will not do for us. However, we can be assured that justice will come when we do not live according to His statutes.

---

[136] John C. Maxwell, *Maxwell Leadership Bible,* (Thomas Nelson, 2007).

The Gibeonites (Joshua 9 and 2 Samuel 21)

The Gibeonites were part of the Hivvite people, original inhabitants of Canaan.[137]After the word spread how God favored Joshua at AI and Jericho, the Gibeonites chose deceit to save themselves from destruction. Disguising themselves as foreign travelers, they ask Joshua for a peace covenant.[138] Joshua made the mistake of not seeking God first and entered the covenant. The ruse is exposed three days later, and the Israelites intend to destroy the Gibeonites. They see the covenant as null and void as it was entered into under false pretenses. Joshua honored the covenant as not to defile God's name. However, Joshua cursed them and made them slaves to the Lord, serving as woodcutters and water carriers for all the congregation.[139] This was the judgment based on the deception of the Gibeonites.

In 2 Samuel 21, David found himself dealing with the Gibeonites due to Saul's war with him. Notice here the subtle judgment from God. David ascended to the throne, and a famine comes over the land for three years. David was concerned that the fam-

---

[137] G. D. Mole, "Cruel Justice, Responsibility, and Forgiveness: On Levinas," *Modern Judaism* 31, no. 3 (2011): 253-271, doi: 10.1093/mj/kjr018.

[138] Joshua 9: 3–6, NKJV

[139] Ibid

ine continued into the third year. David inquired of the Lord and is told, in verse 1, "It is because of Saul and his bloodthirsty house because he killed the Gibeonites."[140] David requested to see the Gibeonites to understand the situation better, only to find that Saul violated the covenant Joshua made with them. The Gibeonites settled in the city of Nob. Saul's massacre of the city included the murder of seven Gibeonites. Survivors of the massacre that served the Kohanim had no livelihood. Saul drove the Gibeonites from the land, killing many in the process. Saul felt he was justified in killing the Gibeonites as members of the Hivvite nation were not entitled to remain in the land of Israel (Joshua 9). Mole stated:

> Saul held that Joshua's covenant with the Gibeonites was invalid. By going against Joshua's promise, ratified as it were by God and the miracle of the sun and the moon, Saul and his family had desecrated God's Name and incurred His wrath. Hence, years later, the famine.[141]

David, realizing the sin against God and the injustice against the Gibeonites, asked how he could atone for Saul's sin. David wanted to be a just king and made

---

[140] G. D. Mole, "Cruel Justice, Responsibility, and Forgiveness: On Levinas," *Modern Judaism* 31, no. 3 (2011): 253-271, accessed May 29, 2023, doi: 10.1093/mj/kjr018.

[141] Ibid, 256

a promise that he would later regret. The Gibeonite's desire for justice did not include any innocent people. They strictly focused on the house of Saul, "invoking the talion law, an eye for an eye." The Gibeonites requested that seven sons of Saul be brought and hanged "for the sake of HaShem in the Gibeah of Saul."[142] David honored the request. According to the exegetist Rakak, "the hanging would show God's justice, for He punished the entire land for three years because of the injustice committed against the Gibeonites."[143]

It is important to note that David spared Mephibosheth, the son of Jonathan. David made an oath to protect and bless Mephibosheth, and did not fulfill one promise at the expense of another. The hanging of the seven descendants of Saul delivered Israel from the sin against the Gibeonites. Mole pointed out the contradiction in Deuteronomy 24:16, which states, "Fathers shall not be put to death for their children, nor shall children be put to death for their fathers; a person shall be put to death for his own sin."[144] Several others bear responsibility, including David. The consensus was this was a heavenly imposed penalty.

---

[142] II Samuel 21:6, NKJV

[143] G. D. Mole, "Cruel Justice, Responsibility, and Forgiveness: On Levinas," *Modern Judaism* 31, no. 3 (2011): 253-271, accessed May 29, 2023, doi: 10.1093/mj/kjr018.

[144] Deuteronomy 24:16, NKJV

God set aside the commandment that sons not be put to death because of their fathers' crimes so that the seven men chosen could atone for Saul's sin.[145]

Notice that Rizpah protected the bodies from Pessach to Sukkot, approximately six months. Mole explained God's decree in the Talmud that the bodies should be left hanging as a lesson that "God condemns those who take advantage of the poor and powerless."[146] This is a powerful visual for everyone. While it may appear harsh, the punishment was proportional to the crime committed against the Gibeonites. Once judgment was rendered and the sentence complete, God heeded the prayers for the land and ended the famine. Guzik pointed out that God will force us to deal with our sin before He continues to answer the prayers of a nation.[147] This is a significant observation given all America is currently experiencing. Could it be, God is waiting for America to deal with her sins?

---

[145] G. D. Mole, "Cruel Justice, Responsibility, and Forgiveness: On Levinas," *Modern Judaism* 31, no. 3 (2011): 253-271, accessed May 29, 2023, doi: 10.1093/mj/kjr018.

[146] Ibid, 257

[147] D. Guzik, Acts 9 - The conversion of Saul of Tarsus," *Enduring Word* (2020).

A Plan for Genocide

Throughout history, the Jews have been the target of numerous attempts at genocide. The Book of Esther is one such attempt. It is the only book in the Bible that does not mention the name of God directly. We do see His handiwork throughout the scriptures. Mayerstein described the Book of Esther as a display of:

> God's absolute power enabling Him to allow our free will and, at the same time, cause that free will to contribute to the realization of His Will on Earth. Ahasuerus' (Xerses) decisions were his own, Haman built his own bed of thorns, and Mordechai and Esther navigated their own courses, yet, perhaps unbeknownst to them, they were operating all the while within the context of God's omnipotence, God's omniscience, and God's omnipresence.[148]

The plot to kill all the Jews was birthed out of Haman's jealousy and outrage that Mordecai did not bow to him.[149] Let us examine why there is such tension between Mordecai and Haman. Haman was a descendant of King Agag, an Amalekite. In Exodus 17:8–16, the Amalekites attacked Israel in Rephidim.

---

[148] Mark A. Mayerstein, *The Book of Esther* (On Demand Publishing, 2018)

[149] Esther 3:5–6, NKJV

Moses directed Joshua to lead Israel's armies against the Amalekites and is victorious as Moses, Aaron, and Hur viewed the battle from the hilltop.[150] God commanded Saul in 1 Samuel 15:1–7 to destroy Amalek to bring final judgment against them for their sins against Israel. Saul disobeyed God, which eventually sealed his fate in losing the throne. Because Saul disobeyed, some descendants of Amalek, like Haman, survived. The consequences of disobedience once again threaten the existence of the Jews.[151]

Haman's rise to power presented concerns for Jews in the kingdom as Haman descended from their mortal enemy. Mordecai's refusal to bow to Haman was the impetus for a planned genocide of the Jewish people. Here we see Haman's desire for carnal justice get the better of him as he seeks retribution against Mordecai and the Jews (Guzik, 2018b). Mayerstein shared his thoughts on Haman's hatred in Esther 3:6 by stating,

> This verse provides a window into the mindset of rabid anti–Semitism. So many times, throughout history, a personal vendetta, valid or not, has morphed into a desire and, more often than not, an effort to destroy the entirety of the Jewish

---

[150] Exodus 17:8–16, NKJV
[151] 1 Samuel 15:1–7, NKJV

population of a region; or even the world. Historically, this has been so common as to be almost cliché.[152]

The proclamation Haman sent throughout the kingdom demanded the annihilation of all the Jews, both young and old, women and children in one day.[153] Mordecai grieved and asked Esther to intercede for her people. Esther was keenly aware of the law and that she had not been summoned by the king. At Mordecai's insistence, Esther requested an audience with the king, as the Jews fasted and prayed with her. In Esther 5:9–13, Haman's anger was stirred against Mordecai at his refusal to bow.[154] Haman concocted a plan to execute Mordecai, even having a gallows constructed. But God intervened, as the king's insomnia kept him up reading the record of the chronicles. Coming across the story of his attempted assassination and Mordecai's loyalty, King Xerses asked Haman how to honor a man that pleases the king. Haman, in his arrogance, thought it was himself. Haman detailed a lavish process to honor such a man and was dumbfounded when the king instructed him to honor Mordecai. Haman's wife and friends saw the writing

---

[152] Mark A. Mayerstein, *The Book of Esther* (On Demand Publishing, 2018).

[153] Esther 3:13, NKJV

[154] Esther 5:9–13, NKJV

on the wall acknowledging that he would not prevail over Mordecai. Even pagans recognized the mighty and just hand of God.[155]

Haman and Xerses attended Ether's second banquet. She made her petition known, asking that her life and the lives of her people be spared. When asked who the guilty party was requiring her life, Esther identified Haman.[156] God justly dealt with Haman as he hung on the very gallows meant for Mordecai. A case of the guilty dying in the place of the innocent.[157]

Saul - A Conversion Like No Other

Let's be clear – Saul was no friend of the church! By all accounts, Saul was the last person anyone would have expected to become its most prominent advocate. We see the skepticism of the church as Saul begins his ministry. Paul had an appetite for persecution. He was present and approved of the stoning of Stephen.[158] Saul saw Christianity as corrupting and twisting his religion, so he set out to bring to justice the

---

155 Esther 5:9–13, NKJV
156 Esther 7:1–6,NKJV
157 D. Guzik, "Esther 7-Haman's End.," *Enduring Word* (2020).
158 Acts 8:1–2, NKJV

heretics who were betraying the God he worshipped his entire life.[159]

Pastor Jim West conducting teaching on Saul, had this to say:

> Saul has great talent, great religious convictions, great intentions. But somewhere along the way, Saul becomes convinced that the Christians are the enemies of God, and with a completely clean conscience, Saul takes on the role of a righteous persecutor. Saul somehow convinced himself that God sanctioned violence in order to preserve religious purity.[160]

Saul thought he was doing the right thing defending his faith in the most zealous way he knew how. His reputation preceded him. The high priest commissioned him to eliminate anyone associated with Christ. Saul was on his way to Damascus to carry out his orders when he encountered Christ. In Acts 9:1–6, we find Saul on the ground answering for his crimes to the one true living God. It is hard not to feel that Saul will get what he deserves for persecuting the

---

[159] D. Limbaugh, "Why Did God Choose the Apostle Paul? ," https://www.thespectrum.com/story/opinion/2018/10/25/why-did-god-choose-apostle-paul/1767491002/

[160] Jim West, "Profile of a Religious Terrorist," https://www.colonialkc.org/sermon-media/2016manuscripts/saul-the-profile-of-a-religious-terrorist/.

Christians.[161] Our humanity wants to see justice. However, it is a carnal view, not a spiritual view. So can you imagine Anania's thoughts when God instructs him to help Saul? Guzik stated, "Ananias' objections were perfectly logical and well–founded. However, they presumed that God needed instruction, or at best, counsel. Ananias almost asked, "God, do you know what kind of guy this Saul is?"[162] I can imaging Ananias asking himself, "What kind of justice is this?" Even amid his fear and doubt, Ananias obeyed the Lord and prayed for Saul. God restored Saul's sight, and he received the Holy Spirit. Paul shared his experience in 1 Timothy 1:13, 16, saying,

> Even though I was once a blasphemer and a persecutor and a violent man, I was shown mercy because I acted in ignorance and unbelief. But for that very reason, I was shown mercy so that in me, the worst of sinners, Christ Jesus might display his immense patience as an example for those who would believe in him and receive eternal life.[163]

Where does justice show up in the life of this former persecutor? I would submit to you that Saul suffered everything that he perpetrated on the early church.

---

[161] Acts 9:1–6, NKJV

[162] D. Guzik, "Acts 9 - The conversion of Saul of Tarsus," *Enduring Word* (2020).

[163] 1 Timothy 1:13, NKJV

Think about all Saul endured in his life after his conversion. Saul shared these trials with us in 2 Corinthians 11:24–28:

> Five times I received from the Jews the forty lashes minus one. Three times I was beaten with rods, once I was pelted with stones, three times I was shipwrecked, I spent a night and a day in the open sea, I have been constantly on the move. I have been in danger from rivers, in danger from bandits, in danger from my fellow Jews, in danger from Gentiles; in danger in the city, in danger in the country, in danger at sea; and in danger from false believers. I have labored and toiled and have often gone without sleep; I have known hunger and thirst and have often gone without food; I have been cold and naked. Besides everything else, I face daily the pressure of my concern for all the churches.[164]

I suppose one could say all that Saul suffered was poetic justice, but that is not how God works. God needed Saul. He broke him and filled him so he could be used for the kingdom. Are we willing to ask Christ, "What do you need me to do, Lord?"

---

[164] 2 Corinthians 11:24–28, NKJV

Judgment Day

In 1991 Arnold Schwarzenegger and Linda Hamilton starred in a sequel of the 1984 movie The Terminator entitled Terminator 2: Judgment Day. The premise for Terminator 2 follows Sarah Connor (Hamilton) and her 10 year old son, John, as they are pursued by a new, more advanced Terminator: the liquid metal, shapeshifting T–1000, sent back in time to kill John and prevent him from becoming the leader of the human resistance. A second, less advanced Terminator (Schwarzenegger) is also sent back in time by the "Resistance" to protect John.[165] Imagine for a moment, Jesus coming back for His bride, the church, while Satan attempts to terminate her.

Written by the Apostle John, the Book of Revelation is an explanation of what happens before, during, and after Christ returns. According to Evans, the Book of Revelation has two goals. First, "to encourage Christians to live righteous and holy lives in light of the prophetic timetable that is to come and secondly, to challenge unbelievers about the judgment ahead if they reject Christ."[166] Growing up, I

---

[165] "The Terminator (1984) Official Trailer - YouTube," *The Terminator*, 1984, video, https://www.youtube.com/watch?v=k64P4l2Wmeg.

[166] Tony Evans, The Tony Evans Study Bible (Nashville : Holman Bible Publishers, 2019).

never wanted to read Revelation. It was a scary book, and quite frankly, I did not understand it. However, I cannot discuss justice and judgment without speaking to the one book that details the end times.

God made it very clear that there will be a reckoning. Malachi 4:1 states, "Surely the day is coming; it will burn like a furnace. All the arrogant and every evildoer will be stubble, and the day that is coming will set them on fire," says the Lord Almighty. "Not a root or a branch will be left to them."[167] This scripture should give us hope that all the injustice transpiring in the world today will be judged by God. Our humanity does not want to hear that. We want to see injustices corrected right now, in our lifetime. If you get nothing else out of this book, remember God has the ultimate plan, and His timing is the only timing that works. We saw 80 years pass as God prepared Moses to deliver the Israelites. Twenty–three years passed before Joseph hit the big stage. Revelation assures us that there will be justice in the long term. Revelation 20:11–15 depicts the final judgment:

> Then I saw a great white throne and him who was seated on it. The earth and the heavens fled from his presence, and there was no place for them. And I saw the dead, great and small, standing

---

[167] Malachi 4:1, NKJV

before the throne, and books were opened. Another book was opened, which is the book of life. The dead were judged according to what they had done as recorded in the books. The sea gave up the dead that were in it, and death and Hades gave up the dead that were in them, and each person was judged according to what they had done. Then death and Hades were thrown into the lake of fire. The lake of fire is the second death. Anyone whose name was not found written in the book of life was thrown into the lake of fire.[168]

The pericope provides insight into the final judgment as those that have accepted Christ enter into eternal life, and those that rejected Him enter eternal damnation. Sound harsh? We have experienced throughout this chapter God's system of justice and to an even greater extent, His mercy. Think about it this way. God knows everything before it happens. He knows the outcome. Yet He still provides everyone an opportunity to "get it right." Warning after warning demonstrates His longsuffering with us and signals His desire for us to follow His perfect plan, to accept Christ. We have a choice to follow or not and, in so doing, determine our own fate on judgment day.

---

[168] Revelation 20:11–15, NKJV

John sees a great white throne where the tri-une God is sitting in authority and power. The color white is representing His purity and holiness. Notice that earth and heaven flee, yet there is no respite for them. Unbelievers will be judged by Christ at the "great white throne" and will be punished according to their works. Romans 2:5 states, "But because of your stubbornness and your unrepentant heart, you are storing up wrath against yourself for the day of God's wrath, when his righteous judgment will be revealed."[169] According to Romans 14:10[170], believers will appear before the "judgment seat of Christ." Death and hades are the last vestiges of sin and they are thrown in the lake of fire.

It is difficult to see the injustices in this world and the oppressor continuing to prosper on the backs of the disenfranchised, the weak, and the poor. There is nothing wrong with righteous indignation; it is what we do with that anger that determines positive or negative outcomes. Fighting injustice is never easy, and at times, it appears no progress is being made. But God is always working either behind the scenes, as in the Book of Esther, or out front leading. Either way, He is a God of justice, and He sees all.

---

[169] Romans 2:5, NKJV
[170] Romans 14:10, NKJV

Enough is Enough - Civil Rights

The ratification of the 13th Amendment abolished slavery in America, but the legislation does not change a heart full of hate. We have already defined biblical justice as a heart issue and conforming to God's moral standard. Unfortunately, everyone does not subscribe to the same moral standard. The roots of Jim Crow began following the ratification of the 13th Amendment and continue to this day albeit, not as overtly. Jim Crow laws were local statutes that legalized racial segregation, limiting Blacks' opportunities in every facet of life. It was a young Dr. King that became the face of the Civil Rights Movement, which started with the Montgomery Bus Boycott from December 5, 1955 – December 20, 1956. Dr. King asked regarding the world's oppressed, "How is the struggle against the forces of injustice to be waged?" He posited two answers: (a) physical violence and (b) corroding hatred or nonviolent resistance.

Dr. King followed the teaching of Mohandas Gandhi, who used nonviolent resistance to "free India from the domination of the British empire."[171] Dr. King detailed the five points to nonviolent resistance first, stating that this is not a method for cowards;

---

[171] Martin Luther King, "Loving Your Enemies - Martin Luther King Speeches," http://www.mlkonline.net/enemies.html.

it does resist. Secondly, nonviolence resistance aims to win the opponent's friendship and understanding, not to humiliate him. Third, the attack is directed against forces of evil, not the individual caught in those forces. Forth, the center of nonviolent resistance is love. Lastly, a conviction that the universe is on the side of justice. There is "a belief that God is on the side of truth and justice comes down to us from the long tradition of our Christian faith."[172] In his letter from a Birmingham jail, Dr. King made it clear to his critics that he was in Birmingham because injustice was there. Likening his visit to the City of Birmingham to the apostles who carried the gospel to the world. The heinous crimes against Blacks in the city of Birmingham were well documented, and Dr. King's letter was a stinging rebuke of those who did not want to get their hands "dirty" in the campaign.

The injustices experienced by Dr. King are a litany of arrests, bombings, stabbing, and eventual assassination. It is reminiscent of Saul's sufferings after his conversion. King's willingness to endure the hardships of a nonviolent campaign with violence hurled at him is an example of how Christ suffered. The recognition that someone has to lead the fight against the injustices of the oppressor and the belief that life for Blacks would change as a result motivat-

---

[172] Ibid, 3

ed Dr. King to continue despite any suffering he may have endured. I believe Dr. King would be sorely disappointed today. While there has been some progress, Jim Crow is still crouching at the door, waiting to block any progress the Black community aspires to achieve. Lincoln and Mamiya articulated the reality that rocks of injustice must be turned over for Blacks to thrive by stating:

> Even before Dr. King's death in 1968, there was a growing realization that the frontier area for the civil rights movement concerned economic justice and equal opportunity. Having the civil right to sit in a restaurant was not enough if a person could not afford to eat there. King's support of the striking sanitation workers in Memphis and his plans for a Poor People's Campaign underscore his vision of the need for economic justice.[173]

The fact that a minister led the Civil Rights Movement is a testament to the Black church and its longevity in supporting the fight against injustice. According to Lincoln and Mamiya, "Black churches were the major mobilization points for mass meetings and demonstrations. Black church members fed and housed the civil rights workers from SNCC, CORE, and other re-

---

[173] C. Eric Lincoln and Lawrence H. Mamiya, *The Black Church in the African American Experience* (Kindle , 2003).

ligious and secular groups."[174] Dr. King was adept at utilizing all available resources and tools to accomplish the vision. There is still much work to be done as a new generation of civil rights activists take the reins. Today's protests and the willingness of so many to trample the rights of others is heartbreaking. Maybe a "more perfect union" is not as close as we thought. There is hope that the sacrifices of those that have gone before will not be in vain. Who will pick up the mantle?

Key Takeaways

- Social justice holds the world view that redistribution is the solution for inequities and inequalities that have attempted to cripple black and brown communities for centuries. Biblical justice is a heart issue and aligns with the law of God. We are children of God, not children of society. Knowing who you are in Christ will change your perspective on justice. Biblical justice rests on the moral authority of biblical principles.

- Justice may not come when we want it, and it may not even come how we expect it, but God will deliver justice.

---

[174] Ibid, 248

- The conversion of Saul demonstrates that change is possible. The church has a responsibility to seek justice where it has become so elusive.

Questions for Reflection and Discussion

1. What is the church's role in influencing social justice reform from a biblical perspective?

____

____

____

____

2. How can your church support social justice activism without compromising its primary mission of winning souls for Christ?

____

____

____

____

GOD PREPARES THE CALLED

"Moreover whom He predestined, these He also called; whom He called, these He also justified; and whom He justified, these He also glorified."[175]

Looking back in history at leaders that led the fight against injustice, I often wondered how they got to that point in their lives. What made them so special? Did they even want to carry the mantle bestowed upon them? God reminds us in Jeremiah 29:11 that He knows the plans for our lives.[176] So when God says, "tag you are it," what do you do? How do you respond? One thing is for sure; God does not do anything halfway. That means there is a level of preparation that will take place over a lifetime to ensure you will meet your destiny at the right time and the right place.

As an Army officer, it took years and thousands of dollars to prepare me to lead some of the world's

---

[175] Romans 8:30, NKJV
[176] Jeremiah 29:11, NKJV

most elite chemical, biological, radiological and nuclear forces. There were numerous courses, exams, obstacles, and evaluations along the way. At the end of each trial, I had a diploma or certificate that signified my ability to lead at the next level. Every new assignment brought about a sense of excitement, but at times, a sense of doubt and skepticism set in causing me to question my ability to lead effectively. How many times have you doubted your ability to achieve a mission all the while knowing you have the training and skills to complete it?

Trust your training. Even in the most difficult of situations, the default is the training you received. However, can you imagine coming face–to–face with the Creator of the universe through a burning bush and being told He chose you to lead the Israelites to freedom? Or imagine being a shepherd boy on the front lines of a battle with a slingshot and five smooth stones facing a terrifying enemy. How do you keep your identity a secret and become the queen of the Persian empire? Would you question your ability to save an entire nation? How do you rebound from persecuting and oppressing the Jews to becoming an apostle of Jesus Christ, writing 13 of the New Testament's 27 books? What would be your reaction at the age of 26 taking on racial injustice in the Jim Crow South? What do these leaders have in common? God chose them for a specific purpose during a particular time in history to exact His will for the kingdom.

How could any of these leaders be sure that their assigned mission would be successful? How could Moses be sure that a nation of people would follow him into the wilderness? How was David so confident in his stand against Goliath? How did Esther face the possibility of death? How did Saul pivot from terror to love on the road to Damascus? And How did Dr. King go forward with protest after protest, knowing the danger that laid ahead for him and his family? We will answer these questions as we examine how God prepared these leaders to meet and fulfill their destinies. The scriptures reveal the preparation and how uniquely qualified they became for the purpose to which God called them. Dr. King utilized the scriptures to show the love of Christ in a nation that showed very little love for people of color.

The church is supposed to be the standard. Romans 12:2 tells us, "do not be conformed to this world."[177] We live here, we work here, but the church should be a reflection of Christ. That means how we define leadership and develop leaders should not mirror the world but the Bible. Biblical leadership, biblical direction, and biblical principles are required. How can the Black church incorporate God's

---

[177] Romans 12:2, NKJV

standard for leadership as they disciple the next generation? Has the church taken a secular or worldly blueprint to build Christian leaders, or are we following a prescription of biblical leadership developed by God? Something to think about as you examine the personalities to follow. I found that self–examination was in order as God revealed my shortcomings as a leader when I take on worldly characteristics versus Godly ones.

Leader and Leadership Defined

Words mean something, so what does it say that the most studied concept has just as many definitions as people that developed them. Studies show 90 variables that comprise the concept of leadership. The only consensus is that there is no consensus on a single definition of leadership. We have an idea of what leadership is, given our worldly experiences while serving as a leader or the recipient of someone else's leadership. Because there are so many variables and theories that attempt to define leadership, no one definition or theory suffices. As a result, some definitions come from the corporate world. Others will quote academia, and others will look to our political system to define leadership. According to Northouse, leadership has the following four components: (a) leadership is a process, (b) leadership involves influence, (c) leadership occurs in groups, and (d) leadership involves common goals. In the secular context, we define leadership as a process whereby an individual influences a group of individuals to achieve a common goal.[178] A leader is the individual or group of individuals executing the process of leadership. Winston and Patterson developed an integrative definition of a leader by stating:

> A leader is one or more people who select, equips, trains, and influences one or more follower(s) who have diverse gifts, abilities, and skills and focuses the follower(s) to the organization's mission and objectives, causing the follower(s) to willingly and enthusiastically expend spiritual, emotional, and physical energy in a concerted, coordinated effort to achieve the organizational mission and objectives.[179]

Ultimately the recurring theme in all definitions of leadership is influence. Maxwell stated, "The true measure of leadership is influence. Nothing more, nothing less."[180] I guess the question is – who and how are leaders influencing followers?

---

[178] Peter G. Northouse, *Leadership Theory and Practice* (SAGE Publications, 2016).

[179] B.E. Winston and K. Patterson, "An Integrative Definition of Leadership," *International Journal of Leadership* (2006): 6-66

[180] John C. Maxwell, *The 21 Irrefutable Laws of Leadership* (Harper Collins, 2007).

Biblical Leadership

The world will continue to develop its spin on leaders and leadership, but what does God say on the subject? If we are going to study leadership, we should consult the original source – the Bible. God established leadership in the Old Testament through the prophets who wielded spiritual authority and were God's mouthpiece. Leaders and the concept of leadership begin in Genesis. *God created man in His image and gave him dominion over the earth.*[181] *God assigned Adam as the head over Eve, providing leadership in their relationship. From the beginning, leadership and leader development are core tenets of God's intent and design. Ayers defined a biblical leader is a person of character and competence who influences a community of people to achieve a God–honoring calling through Christ's power.* Ayers also defined biblical leadership as God–oriented and people–focused. Biblical leaders acknowledge the presence of God in their leadership. He is the foundation. [182]

Leadership development and training programs in today's society are designed to produce outcomes

---

[181] Genesis 1:27-28 NKJV

[182] Mike Ayers, *Power to Lead: Five Essentials for the Practice of Biblical Leadership* , Kindle Edition (Spring: RBK Publishing, 2015).

– quantitative results. In contrast, biblical leaders desire to obey God and leave the results up to Him. Biblical leadership is measured first in terms of faithfulness, what God wants, and then what it seeks to accomplish for people to the glory of God.[183] Biblical leaders seek quantitative results, which include discipleship, service, and demonstrating love.

Leaders do not develop in a day. It takes a lifetime.[184] God develops leaders over time, guiding them through obstacles and trials, trying them in the crucible if you will. Building leaders is a process, and there is no better process than God's. We do not always enjoy the process, but it is necessary to support His intent for the kingdom.

To understand how God develops leaders, I will utilize the power to lead model developed by Ayers). Admittedly, Northouse's four components could include Ayer's five principles except for God as the foundation. Ayers described five leadership principles that emerge in every leader God calls, which include: (a) character, (b) calling, (c) competence, and (d) community, with (e) Christ as the foundation. Let's examine the development of God's chosen through

---

[183] Mike Ayers, *Power to Lead: Five Essentials for the Practice of Biblical Leadership* , Kindle Edition (Spring: RBK Publishing, 2015).

[184] John C. Maxwell, *Leadership 101* (HarperCollins Leadership, 2002).

the lens of the power to lead Model. Ayers defined these terms as we apply them to the lives of Moses, King David, Esther, Dr. King, Paul, and Jesus.[185]

Character

The Old Testament defines character (esheth chayil) as meaning the power that flows from within and may denote one who is virtuous. In the New Testament, the most common Greek word for the concept of character is dokime (δοκιμη). The word study dictionary describes the word as "proving, trial, approved, tried character; a proof, specimen of tried worth."[186]

Calling to Lead and Influence

Ayers defined a call to lead as a unique prompting of God to be used by him to influence others to achieve some kind of God–honoring future. Ayers described the calling to influence can be achieved by being used where you are and as you are through the power of personal leadership.[187]

---

[185] Mike Ayers, *Power to Lead: Five Essentials for the Practice of Biblical Leadership* , Kindle Edition (Spring: RBK Publishing, 2015).
[186] Ibid, 48
[187] Ibid, 77

Competence

Do you know what you are doing? If you do not, it is a matter of time before you look back, and no one is following. Your character may be above reproach, and the call on your life strong. Still, without competent execution of core skillsets and proper utilization of assigned gifts and talents, no one will follow you. Those core skills include: (a) effectively communicating, (b) creating a thriving culture, (c) leading change, (d) resolving conflict, and (e) developing those you lead. If you can do all that while identifying and operating in your spiritual gifts and natural competencies, you will be a force for transformative change.

Community

Leaders must focus on the people. Ayers asked a crucial question – are leaders managing things or leading people? Building a Christian community is at the heart of biblical leadership. Suppose leaders lead from a place of love. In that case, people thrive, benefit, and are best influenced by the power of the Christian community. The outcome of biblical leadership is always about transforming the lives of human beings.[188]

---

[188] Ibid

Christ: The Power of the Leader

The bottom line up front – we need more, Jesus! When we have Jesus, we have more power. This power is the indwelling of the Holy Spirit. How can we be biblical leaders without a personal relationship with Christ?[189] All the other principles flow from the foundation of Christ. Think of it this way. A leader's character is shaped by the experiences the Father leads him through. The call originates with the Father as He introduces them to their destiny. The skills and gifts endowed to develop a competent leader comes from the Father. Lastly, the world is the community we serve, commanded by Christ to bring individuals to the body and disciple them in the ways of Christ.

The scriptures are full of men and women God called to a specific purpose. He does not call the qualified; He qualifies the called. Do you identify with these biblical heroes? What has God called you to, and can you see His fingerprints all over your development? This chapter will focus on how God prepared and used the least likely to address the injustices of their time.

---

[189] Ibid

Moses - Chosen Deliverer

Pharaoh's unfounded fear of an overthrow led to the Hebrew people's unjust enslavement and oppression. Given the complexities in liberating the Hebrews from Egypt, God had to select the right person to confront Pharaoh. God prepared Moses for 80 years for the task of freeing His people. Seemingly insignificant acts are huge supporting pillars in God's plan for Moses. God addressed the injustice of Hebrew enslavement by multiplying the nation. The more Pharaoh oppressed, the more the nation grew. The faithfulness of two midwives, Shiphrah and Puah, allowed the Hebrew population to multiply so quickly that Pharoah feared the Hebrews would rise against him. This fear perpetuated the death of all male Hebrew children. [190]

Pharaoh's genocide, a cruel act of population control and oppression, did not arise based on race, but Pharaoh's fear that the Hebrews would one day align with the state's enemies and overtake the Egyptians. It was purely a social and economic decision. Moses, by all accounts, should have been dead.[191] We see by design how God orchestrated Moses' arrival in Pharaoh's palace. His "adoption" by Pharaoh's daugh-

---

[190] Exodus 1: 9–10, NKJV
[191] Exodus 1, NKJV

ter, Hatshepsut, provide him with the educational and developmental opportunities that would come to bear in the confrontation with Pharaoh some 40 years later.

God is constantly developing the character of His people. Moses was no exception. The development of character includes the education, training, and personal experiences in one's journey. Therefore, the other components of Ayers' model, calling, competence, and community, contribute to building and solidifying a person's character. Moses was a man of humility. Numbers 12:3 characterized Moses as very meek, "now the man Moses was very humble, more than all men that were on the face of the earth."[192] We know from his years of shepherding that he was a hard worker. He developed a sense of justice, a moral compass that eventually led to his 40 year exile. Moses was passionate and impulsive, which contributed to God denying him entry into the Promised Land. Yet it is that same passion that God valued as Moses passionately intercedes for Israel.[193]

Stephen spoke to Moses' competence in Acts 7:22, stating, "Moses was learned in all the wisdom of the Egyptians and was mighty in words and

---

[192] Numbers 12:3, NKJV
[193] Exodus 32:9–14, NKJV

deeds."[194] As a result, Moses received exposure to Egyptian culture. He learned how to read and write Egyptian dialects as well as understand hieratic and hieroglyphic systems. Moses' training and education in communication set him on a path to write the Pentateuch. He would have learned foreign languages and become proficient in mathematics. His training in social, political, and geographical areas undoubtedly helped Moses interact with various people encountered on the way to the Promise Land.

God moved Moses' heart to visit his brethren. Moses intervened in the beating of a Hebrew brother and kills the Egyptian oppressor. He was unaware that his crime became public knowledge. He was confronted and escaped to Midian to begin the next phase of his leadership training. Over the next 40 years, God developed Moses' character as a shepherd working for his father–in–law. A stark contrast from his life in an Egyptian palace.

Moses continued to develop his sense of justice and fairness as he regularly intervened for those who could not protect themselves as he did with Reuel's (Jethro) daughters.[195] Moses married Zipporah and raised two sons, and settled into life as a shepherd in Median. Preparation for the shepherding of a na-

---

194 Acts 7:22, NKJV
195 Exodus 2:17, NKJV

tion. The significance of shepherding cannot be understated. Moses learned the roles and functions of a shepherd as God prepared him for the most challenging mission of his life.

Shepherds are caring, demonstrate courage and deliver guidance. Moses performed these functions as he led the Israelites to freedom. The training program, if you will, included a detailed understanding of each function. The caring function includes restoration, feeding, watering, grooming, shearing, delivering lambs, leading, and protection. The function of courage focuses on activities of assuming responsibility, serving, and participating in change. The guidance function gives a particular highlight on hodegos [leader or guide] – to lead or guide concerning a decision or future course of action. Most of the time, we have no idea we are training for God's bigger picture. After 40 years of shepherding, God certified Moses' ability to shepherd the Hebrews through one of the most challenging times in Israel's history.

Moses' call to duty takes place on Mount Horeb. The Lord appeared to Moses as a burning bush not consumed by the fire.[196] Why did God appear as a burning bush? Was it to get Moses' attention, or was there some other intention behind this theophany? There are several theories regarding why God chose

---

[196] Exodus 3:2, NKJV

to reveal himself to Moses in this manner. A Google search stated fire is mentioned 510 times in scripture. It either destroys or purifies (Adamo, 2017). In this case, the fire purified the ground, thus the command for Moses to remove his sandals, for he was standing on holy ground. God displayed his holiness like never before as He formally advised Moses of his call.

Imagine being 80 years old and told by "I AM" that you will deliver the Hebrews out of Egypt. At this moment, the call revealed aspects of Moses' character as well as God's. Moses listed five excuses why he could not lead. However, Moses' excuses did not change God's mind about Moses' ordained purpose. We see a humble man, yet Moses had a self–esteem issue.

1. Who am I? Moses did not feel qualified. He questioned his identity in God. God responded, "I am with you."[197]

2. Who are you? Moses did not know God well. There was a lack of relationship. God responded, "I AM WHO I AM."[198]

3. What if they don't listen? Moses was intimidated and concerned about what the people

197 Exodus 3:12, NKJV
198 Exodus 3:14, NKJV

thought. God gives him direction in performing miracles.[199]

4. I do not speak well. God responds, "Who has made man's mouth? I will be with you."[200]

5. Can you send someone else? Moses felt inadequate for the job. God responds by allowing Aaron to go with him but emphasizes Moses is the called.[201]

That brings us to the fourth component in the model – community. God tasked Moses with leading the Hebrew nation of approximately 20,000 people out of Egypt.[202] Jealousy drove a new king to disregard the Hebrew nation's contributions to Egypt's cultural and economic success. Pharaoh enslaved and oppressed them. When Moses returned to Egypt, the Hebrew community had been enslaved for 400 years.[203]

God will use various experiences and circumstances to ensure His people are ready to assume their missions. God took 80 years to prepare Moses,

---

[199] Exodus 4:2–9, NKJV

[200] Exodus 4:11–12, NKJV

[201] Exodus 4:14–17, NKJV

[202] C.J. Humphreys, "The Number of People in the Exodus from Egypt: Decoding Mathematically the Very Large Numbers in Numbers I and XXI." *Vetus Testamentum* (1998): 200.

[203] Gen 15:13, NKJV

a reminder that developing good leaders is a process. Most of us would be well into our retirement. Moses was a product of his experiences and environment. Being raised in Pharaoh's house provided insight into the Egyptian way of life. In developing Moses' character, God provided him the means and opportunity to become a competent leader. God then called him to a seemingly impossible task for a specific community, all the while leading and guiding him through each trial. Over time, Moses' faith increased, his confidence grew, but Moses' "superpower," if you will, was his obedience to God. Moses was not perfect, but he was the tool God used to free His people from slavery.

David - A Leader after God's Heart

Learning King David's life, many a Sunday school student has asked, how could God use such a man? He was so flawed. A liar, adulterer, and murderer, to name a few of his issues. But what better way for God to show His glory than to use David's life as an example of redemption and purpose? The life of David is a study in leadership development and preparation. God tells us he chose David because he was a man after His own heart, "and the Lord had commanded him to be commander over His people."[204]

---

[204] 1 Samuel 13:14, NKJV

The prophet Samuel anointed David king of Israel between the ages of 10 and 15 years old. However, he did not ascend to the throne until he was 30. What was God doing with David in those 15 to 20 years before he became king? Jesse, the youngest of eight boys, considered David irrelevant and was tending the sheep when Samuel arrived to anoint the next king of Israel. Here again, just as with Moses, God used the shepherding profession to develop David's character, competence, and trust in God.

How does an individual become a man or woman after God's own heart? David's mother raised him in the admonition of the Lord. He had a relationship with God at an early age. The shepherding experience afforded David an abundance of time to spend with God, which strengthened their relationship. God called David out of the field, tending sheep to be the next king of Israel. He used the shepherding experience to develop a shepherd's heart, one of caring and concern that would come to bear in shepherding the Israelites during his reign. During his time in the fields, David struck down both the lion and the bear.[205] His ability to defeat both prepared him for the eventual meeting with Goliath. These brave acts instilled in David a level of confidence that he could conquer anything before him with the help of the

---

[205] I Samuel 17:35–36, NKJV

Lord. His faith in God continued to grow with each trial.

God continued to prepare David for his reign as Israel's king as he gained entrance to the palace as the psalmist that could calm the tormenting demon in Saul. If God allowed David to ascend to the throne directly after his anointing, David would not be competent to serve, not understanding the varying facets of being a king. In serving Saul, David learned royal etiquette and how to rule the people, and the negatives of Saul's rule. David became Saul's armor–bearer giving him access to military knowledge and training.[206] Much like Moses, exposure to the palace as a training ground developed David's confidence and competence.

Killing Goliath increased David's popularity among the people. Again a hand of favor from God in preparing not only David for the throne but also the people. David's character was such that the people's praise did not affect his humility. As a result, Saul became singularly focused on killing David. Yet, David was wise, disciplined, and obedient to the Spirit of the Lord. David had several opportunities to kill Saul. However, in obedience to God, he spared Saul's life.

---

[206] R.L. Deffinbaugh, "David's Youth: A Training Ground for Godly Leadership," https://bible.org/seriespage/1-davids-youth-training-ground-godly-leadership.

David chose to run versus confront Saul. There is a purpose in the running. For seven years, David ran from Saul. It was not yet time for David to ascend to the throne. He realized he must wait on God. David was in a testing period, learning to trust God no matter what the circumstances were.

All the adversity David faced prepared him to become king of the Hebrew community. David was not perfect by any stretch of the imagination, but he had a heart and love for God like no other. His passion for the people mirrored his passion for God. During David's seven year cat and mouse with Saul, God called 400 men to David. The distressed, the broke, and discounted gathered at the Addullum Cave where David took command over them. These men became a rebel army against Saul.[207] As broken as these men were when they arrived, David developed them into "Mighty men of valor, men trained for battle, who could handle the shield and spear, whose faces were like the faces of lions, and were as swift as gazelles on the mountains.[208] David had compassion and love for these men – a community that he influenced to become warriors for justice. God does not leave a developing leader alone or to face battles by

---

[207] D. Guzik, "David at the Adullam Cave, Saul Murders the Priests," https://enduringword.com/bible-commentary/1%20Samuel%2022/.

[208] 1 Chronicles 12:8, NKJV

themselves. He will surround them with people and resources to support them.

David's superpower was his repentant heart. When he recognized his lies cost the lives of the priests in Nob, he repented. After his infidelity with Bathsheba and the murder of her husband, Uriah, David repented. David wanted to please God. He was accountable for the people well before he took the throne. God made his choice early and developed David to be an effective leader for the people of Israel.

Esther - For Such a Time as This

The story of Esther is another example of how God prepares an individual for their eventual calling. He is not overt about it, yet we see His hand in every detail of Esther's story. Esther was an orphan raised by her cousin Mordecai. He raised her to be kind, gracious, respectful, and love the Lord. Esther loved her family and her people and accepted the call with humility and courage to deliver the Jews. Before being presented to the king, the 12 months of training gave Esther insight into the palace's inner workings and knowledge of Persian law. She found favor with Hegai and, in her wisdom, conferred with him in the processes of pleasing the king.

There is an intersection of leaders and leadership in Esther's story. Mordecai served as an excellent example for Esther. He saved the King's life when he became aware of an assassination attempt and shared the information. Esther observed Mordecai maintaining his moral code by not bowing down to Haman. Mordecai's disobedience to the decree sparked Haman's anger, and he plotted to kill the Jewish people. Mordecai instilled, via observation, a sense of responsibility for more than himself in Esther. Mordecai did not stay in the shadows. He came forth to expose a plot and then demonstrated loyalty, faith, and love for God in not adhering to a decree to bow to Haman. Mordecai's actions shaped Esther's character as she learned duty, honor, and devotion to God.

Queen Vashti's expulsion set things in motion for Esther to be in the right place at the right time to save the Jewish nation from Haman's planned genocide. From a cultural perspective, men expected women to do what they were told. Vashti underestimated her husband's response to her perceived disrespect. King Xerses wanted to ensure women stayed in their place and men ruled their homes. Vashti became the example. God used this unfortunate incident to elevate Esther to the throne.

Esther's call was a bit more subtle than Moses' and David's. God used Mordecai to guide and instruct Esther after the death of her parents. When Esther was selected to go before the king, Mordecai told Esther to keep her ethnicity a secret. After Haman threatened the Jews, Mordecai urged Esther to step forward and reveal her ethnicity, ultimately saving the Jewish state. In all Esther did, she attained favor with man and God, as she leveraged opportunities to influence outcomes.

In response to Haman's decree to kill all Jewish people, Mordecai tore his clothes and wore sackcloth and ashes. Haman cast lots to determine the timeline for this heinous act. Mordecai asked Esther to intercede for the people with King Xerxes, to which she replied that she had not seen her husband in 30 days. Esther quoted the law back to Mordecai, making it clear that she had not been summoned and faced death should King Xerxes not extend the scepter.[209] Notice how Mordecai held Esther accountable:

> Do not think in your heart that you will escape in the king's palace any more than all the other Jews. For if you remain completely silent at this time, relief and deliverance will arise for the Jews from another place, but you and your father's house will perish. Yet who knows whether

---

[209] Esther 4:11, NKJV

you have come to the kingdom for such a time as this?[210]

Esther understood the power of prayer and fasting, requiring the Jewish people to do so for three days before meeting with the king. Esther devised a plan to invite the King and Haman to a feast where she planned to intercede for her people. Esther was sensitive to the Holy Spirit and responded to His guidance after the first feast realizing the timing was not suitable to make her request. Esther was determined to be obedient to her call. Therefore she planned a second feast. Her statement, "If I perish, I perish," demonstrated courage in the face of adversity.

Esther was chosen initially for appearance, beauty versus credentials. However, she was not just another pretty face.[211] Esther pled for her life and interceded for her people. The wisdom to ensure Haman was present maximized the impact on the king as he realized Haman plotted to kill his wife.

Esther's faith in God and her willingness to submit to the wisdom provided by Mordecai and Hegai eventually led her to become queen. Her courage and willingness to die to save her community is a

---

[210] Esther 2:13–14, NKJV

[211] S.G. Davis, "Esther Position Power Person Power, Gifts," https://godgiftsyou.com/blog/2019/3/13/calling-and-purpose-8estherposition-power-personal-power-gifts.

selfless act. Esther's influence grew and according to Esther 9:29, she "wrote with full authority."[212] Esther issued a decree confirming Purim. For Esther to wield that much authority in a culture that minimized women was particularly impressive. As a result of the favor on her life, Esther gained power and wealth for Mordecai as he became second in command only to King Xerxes. Esther's superpower was her obedience to what God called her to and the courage to follow through. Although there were no bright flashing lights, bells, or whistles going off, God chose Esther for such a time as this!

Saul/Paul - From Terrorist to Apostle

The Google dictionary defines a terrorist as a person who uses unlawful violence and intimidation, especially against civilians, in the pursuit of political aims. In the case of Saul, we can add religious obsession to the definition. Born in Tarsus, Saul came from a prominent family. His father was a Pharisee. Saul was considered a prodigy. He was well educated, spoke three languages, highly esteemed, influential, intelligent, and was passionate and extremely loyal to his Jewish convictions.

---

[212] Esther 9:29, NKJV

As with the other heroes discussed thus far, God already had a plan for Saul. Even the names Saul and Paul are significant. Saul was a Jewish name used by the family, and Paul was his Roman name, used by non–Jews in his hometown. The fact that this Hellenistic–Jewish boy has two names – a Jewish name and a Gentile name foreshadowed the role he would play in spreading the gospel to the Gentiles.[213] His dual–citizenship allowed him to fit into both worlds. Although Saul was not aware of the call on his life at the time, God orchestrated every detail to transform him from a terror to an apostle. Paul wrote to the Galatians, "but when it pleased God, who separated me from my mother's womb and called me through His grace, to reveal His Son in me, that I might preach Him among the Gentiles."[214] The call and the community were ordained by God before Paul was born.

So why did God allow such carnage to go on in the name of religion? Could God have converted Saul at the stoning of Stephen and been just as effective? Of course, He could, but God is constantly revealing His character while transforming ours, or in this case, Paul's character. Piper (2012) published

---

[213] Jim West, "Profile of a Religious Terrorist," https://www.colonialkc.org/sermon-media/2016manuscripts/saul-the-profile-of-a-religious-terrorist/.

[214] Galatians 1:15–16, NKJV

an article listing six reasons why God allowed these atrocities to occur.

1. To put the perfect patience of Christ on display. "I received mercy for this reason, that in me, as the foremost, Jesus Christ might display his perfect patience."[215]

2. To encourage those who think they are too sinful to have hope. "I received mercy for this reason, that in me, as the foremost, Jesus Christ might display his perfect patience *as an example to those who were to believe in him for eternal life.*"[216]

3. To show that God saves hardened haters of Christ, who have even murdered Christians.

4. To show that God permits his much–loved elect to sink into flagrant wickedness.

5. To show that God can make the chief of sinners the chief of missionaries.

6. To show a powerless, persecuted, marginalized church that they can triumph by the supernatural conversion of their most powerful foes. (p. 1-2)

---

[215] 1 Timothy 1:16, NKJV
[216] Ibid

Leadership is about influence, whether good or bad, and Saul had influence. Many followed Saul in the persecution of Christians. Stephen's stoning in Acts 7 was a horrific act by the Sanhedrin, and Saul admitted that he took pleasure in Stephen's death. How could someone so highly educated take pleasure in the savage killing of another human being? Saul described his upbringing and his heart toward God; "I am indeed a Jew, born in Tarsus of Cilicia, but brought up in this city (Jerusalem) at the feet of Gamaliel, taught according to the strictness of our fathers' law, and was zealous toward God as you all are today."[217] Saul's character at this time was described as prideful, driven, and fiercely loyal to his Jewish convictions and heritage. Saul regretted his brutality persecuting the church. He stated in Acts 26:11, "And I punished them often in every synagogue and compelled them to blaspheme; and being exceedingly enraged against them, I persecuted them even to foreign cities."[218]

Saul had great intentions concerning his beliefs. He became convinced that Christians are the enemies of God, and his mission was to stop the spread of false religions. Under this mindset, Saul's conscience was clear as he believed he was doing God's will in

---

[217] Acts 22:3, NKJV
[218] Acts 26:11, NKJV

eliminating Christians. The same character traits that made Saul obsessive and ruthless are the same traits God used after Paul's conversion to spread the word to the Gentiles. Paul's awakening on the Damascus road removed the pride and replaced it with humility. There is no doubt that Paul pursued Christ with the same passion he had in persecuting and killing Christ's followers. Paul's superpower was his passion for the gospel.

According to Ayers' biblical leadership model, Saul exhibited four of the five principles of a biblical leader even before conversion. He lacked a relationship with Christ until after his conversion. What is important to remember is not who Paul was but who he became. Biblical leadership is about transforming lives. Anytime God calls forth a leader for a task, His purpose is to redeem and restore His people.[219] God will start with the leader himself. Paul's leadership was God–enabled, Spirit–led, word–based, cross–shaped, and deeply relational. Paul was an example for believers to follow. When he talked about the importance of suffering, Paul was a credible testimony. God selected, prepared, and equipped Paul to be an apostle (Smith, 2014). God does not hold a demo-

---

[219] Mike Ayers, *Power to Lead: Five Essentials for the Practice of Biblical Leadership* , Kindle Edition (Spring: RBK Publishing, 2015).

cratic process to select leaders. God's "thoughts and ways are not our thoughts and ways."[220] Given Saul's early reputation, I am sure we would agree that none of us would choose Saul to lead anyone. That is why God does the choosing. He looks at the whole life, not just the undesirable areas.

Dr. Martin Luther King - Reluctant Servant

Dr. Martin Luther King Jr., pastor, Nobel Peace Prize winner, and most notably, leader of the Civil Rights Movement. Dr. King is arguably one of the most historical personalities in history. While not a biblical figure, Dr. King subscribed to the biblical principles of leadership. Dr. King followed in the footsteps of his father and grandfather, ministers of the gospel and pastors of Ebenezer Baptist Church in Atlanta, Georgia. As a minister, he understood what a calling meant and the responsibility and accountability God requires. Dr. King took a Christ–centered approach toward injustice and modeled for the black community how to follow Christ in an unjust society. Dr. King acknowledged his call to root out injustice in his "Letter from Birmingham Jail." In answering the criticisms of clergy within the city of Birmingham, King (1963) held himself accountable to his call, stating,

---

[220] Isaiah 55:8, NKJV

> I am in Birmingham because injustice is here. Just as the prophets of the eighth century B.C. left their villages and carried their "thus saith the Lord" far beyond the boundaries of their home towns, and just as the Apostle Paul left his village of Tarsus and carried the gospel of Jesus Christ to the far corners of the Roman world, so am I compelled to carry the gospel of freedom beyond my own hometown. Like Paul, I must constantly respond to the Macedonian call for aid. [221]

Dr. King reminded his critics (eight White clergymen) that "he is like them, "a religious leader looking to spread the gospel of peace and community."[222]

At the age of 26, Dr. King became a reluctant leader of a Civil Rights movement that shook the nation to its core. Dr. King possessed several character traits that made him a successful transformational leader. He was intelligent. An avid reader, Dr. King continued to hone his intellectual skills through formal and informal education. Dr. King was diligent in his non–violent methodology, choosing to follow the teachings of Jesus Christ. He displayed bravery in the face of physical and verbal attacks. As a gifted orator, Dr. King motivated followers to "buy–in" to

---

[221] Martin Luther King, "Letters from Birmingham Jail," www.liberationcurriculum.org.

[222] G. Sheriff, "Letter from Birmingham Jail," https://litcharts.com.

the dream God had shown him. A visionary, able to articulate the big picture, and dedicated himself to leading through the storm. He never succumbed to a violent solution.

Like Moses, God called Dr. King to lead a people out of an unjust society into a promised land of equality and opportunity. There is a level of competence required to accomplish this task. Dr. King was well educated and surrounded himself with individuals that offered sound advice and guidance. He studied Mahatma Gandhi's principle of "Satyagraha." This principle is based upon truth, governments by consensus, persuasion through decision and reason, education of the community, decisive action, and mass civil disobedience. According to Gardner , there are seven forms of intellect, which include: (a) linguistic, (b) logical–mathematical, (c) musical, bodily–kinesthetic, (d) spatial, (e) interpersonal, and (f) intrapersonal. King demonstrated genius in three forms of intellect, which included: (a) linguistic, (b) interpersonal, and (c) intrapersonal.[223] Dr. King's competence extended to innovative technologies like the television to speak to larger crowds. Broadcasting the movement helped make the rest of the country aware of the atrocities suffered by the Black community.

---

[223] Howard Gardner, *Frames of Mind: The Theory of Multiple Intelligences* (New York: Basic Books, 1983).

On the surface, it appears Dr. King was singularly called to the Black community. I would argue that God called him to stir the consciousness of the body of Christ. Tisby addressed the fact that Christian moderates—primarily White and evangelical and some Black churches and ministers, played it safe and refused to get involved in the civil rights movement. These people of faith may not have given their full support to the most extreme racists; however, they did not oppose racists outright or openly disagree with racist objectives. Very few Christians publicly aligned themselves with the struggle for Black freedom in the 1950s and 1960s. There was a backlash from families, friends, and fellow Christians for those who supported the civil rights movement. At a critical moment in our nation's history, one that called for moral courage, the American church responded to much of the civil rights movement with passivity, indifference, or outright opposition.[224]

Christian leaders, leading biblically, are sorely needed as this nation continues to struggle with injustice. The leaders discussed in this chapter are examples of Ayers' power to lead model focused on biblical leadership. Unfortunately, today we have a crisis of leadership. Tripp is optimistic about the local

---

[224] Jemar Tisby, *The Color of Compromise* (Grand Rapids : Zondervan, 2019).

church. But he is concerned that "behind a pastor's failure is a weak and failed leadership community. We don't have just a pastoral crisis; we have a leadership crisis."[225] So, if we have a leadership crisis, who will be the voice in the wilderness to cry out and stand against injustice?

Key Takeaways

- Current leadership development and training programs focus on producing outcomes – quantitative results. In contrast, Biblical leaders desire to obey God, seeking quantitative results, including discipleship, service, and demonstrating love. The difference between worldly leadership and *biblical* leadership is God.

- God qualifies the called. His process may take decades. However, the life experiences culminate in developing a leader that God can use for His purposes.

- Leadership is influence. Someone is always watching a leader's actions and reactions. We learn from Moses the importance of identity and its development in the heart of a leader. We observe Esther's courage to lead despite significant risk. David demonstrates the life and power available

---

[225] P.D. Tripp, *Lead* (Crossway: Wheaton , 2020).

for leaders who develop intimacy with God. God shows the forgiveness available for leaders when moral failure occurs. In Paul, we witness the credibility and trust gained through hard work and spiritual passion. While Dr. King is not a biblical figure, he is a biblical leader. We learn from his walk the importance of having a vision.

- Each of these leaders accepted the call on their lives. The preparation, at times, was arduous and unwelcomed. The mission may have seemed impossible, and the sacrifices unbearable. They had the heart to do God's will regardless of what it might cost them. That is biblical leadership! God always promises to walk with us. If he calls us to it, He will walk us through the challenges we face.

Questions for Reflection and Discussion

Have your leaders take the Gift Test which can gifttest.org. Discuss the results.

1. How is your church selecting and developing leaders?

____

____

____

2. Now that each leader understands their gifts, are they placed in positions to be successful in their call?

____

____

____

____

3. Are you a leader after God's own heart?

____

____

____

____

4. Identify your fears in leading and your plans to overcome them.

____

____

____

____

THE BLACK CHURCH - INFLUENTIAL OR NOT?

She [The Black Church] has endured the most racially oppressive times in the dark history of the United States, and when humanity was stripped from blacks, pastors and deacons in the Black Church proclaimed Scripture in a way that reaffirmed that all men were created in the image of God and slaves, like other men, were valued in God's sight.[226]

The Black church has weathered many a storm in its lifetime. However, there is a narrative that says the Black church is dead. The church is no longer the epicenter of Black communities. Does it continue to be, as in days gone by, the center of the Black community? Lincoln and Mamiya stated:

The Black Church has no challenger as the cultural womb of the black community. Not only did it give birth to new institutions such as schools,

---

[226] E. I. Grant, "The Witness - BCC," accessed May 29, 2023, https://thewitnessbcc.com/.

banks, insurance companies, and low–income housing, it also provided an academy and an arena for political activities, and nurtured young talent for musical, dramatic, and artistic development.[227]

The criticism is often brutal as activist leaders throughout the community chastise the Black church for lack of involvement in urban areas and inner cities. Is the criticism warranted? Maybe so, in some respects. A new generation is rising, and they do not wholly subscribe to how the "old establishment" navigates today's hot button issues. They say, "don't talk about it, be about it!' It is a call to action, not just prayers, and hymns but a concerted effort to fight and provide support in all areas of the Black community where injustice may be lurking. It is these concerns that have sparked the conversation that the Black church is dead. But do we throw the baby out with the bathwater? Or do we look for ways and opportunities to join forces to be inclusive without minimizing the institution that has been the epicenter for an oppressed people for centuries? Du Bois stated, "practically, a proscribed people must have a social Centre, and that Centre for this

---

[227] C. Eric Lincoln and Lawrence H. Mamiya, *The Black Church in the African American Experience* (Duke University Press, 2003).

people is the Negro church."[228] Lincoln and Mamiya supported this line of thinking, stating, "We suspect that Black churches, on the whole, are more socially active in their communities than white churches and that they also tend to participate in a greater range of community programs."[229] But is this true today?

As I watched the runoff election results pour in from the state of Georgia, I could not help but reminisce on time spent in Griffin, Georgia. My mom and grandmother were the centers of my life while my father went to war in Vietnam. The church was a force in my life, as was the community that never let me get away with anything. We attended Heck Chapel on 2nd Street. I remember my brother and I sitting on the front pew, legs swinging back and forth as mom sang in the choir and grandma played the organ and piano. I was proud of the Black community in Georgia as I saw the Black church's impact on the election results. A black minister stood triumphant as the newest member of the United States Senate.

Raphael Warnock is the first African American senator from the state of Georgia. It is a truly historic moment in time as there have only been 11 Blacks

---

[228] W. E. B. Dubois, *The Souls of Black Folk* (Tampa: Millenium Publications , 1903).

[229] C. Eric Lincoln and Lawrence H. Mamiya, *The Black Church in the African American Experience* (Duke University Press, 2003).

elected to the senate – 11 in 232 years. According to historian Eric Foner, "three of the first 16 African American members of Congress were ministers, and of the more than 2,000 Black officeholders at every level of government in that era, more than 240 were ministers—second only to farmers."[230] There is no doubt that the Black community looked to the Black church for leadership to represent their interest in legislative bodies nationwide. The Black church always has been in the mix concerning politics and the impact elections have on the Black community. The Black church has always been a place that birthed leaders unapologetically Black and Christian willing to carry the mantle of freedom. The Black church has a history of ushering in change and standing for justice. So why is the current conversation predicting the demise of the Black church?

The Black Church is Dead

In 2010, Dr. Glaude penned a piece in the Huffington Post where he posited that the Black church is dead. As you can imagine, it raised quite a stir. He detailed three reasons for his remarks. First, we must acknowledge a conservative dimension of Black Christian

---

[230] Henry Louis Gates, "To Understand America, You Need to Understand the Black Church," https://time.com/5939921/ henry-lous-gates-american-history-black-church/.

life that never comes to the forefront of discussion. Second, he went against the traditional mindset that the Black church is the center of Black communities. Glaude stated:

> Different areas of black life have become more distinct and specialized — flourishing outside of the bounds and gaze of black churches. I am not suggesting that black communities have become wholly secular, just that black religious institutions and beliefs stand alongside a number of other vibrant non–religious institutions and beliefs.[231]

He spoke to the departure of members from predominantly Black churches to congregations like Joel Osteen, Rick Warren, and Jentzen Franklin. Thirdly, we spend too much time looking back. A preoccupation with past endeavors tends to distract what the church should be doing or how it should respond in the future. The result is a church that has lost power. What is the role of the Black church in addressing injustices and the economic and political aspects of black life? Dr. Glaude left us with this though:

> Any church as an institution ought to call us to be our best selves — not to be slaves to doctrine or mere puppets for profit. Within its walls,

---

[231] E. Glaude, "The Black Church Is Dead ," https://www.huffpost.com/entry/the-black-church-is-dead_b_473815.

our faith should be renewed and refreshed. We should be open to experiencing God's revelation anew. But too often, we are told that all has been said and done. Revelation is closed to us, and we should only approximate the voices of old. Rare are those occasions when black churches mobilize *in public and together* to call attention to the pressing issues of our day.[232]

Butler in a lecture to The United Lutheran Seminary, stated, "the black church is on life support right now; it's in a coma, the fact of the matter is, you don't have any of these kids in your church."[233]we expect the next generation to act and think as we do. However, millennials look at the world through very different lenses. A new Barna study conducted in 2021 did not necessarily negate the view that the Black church is the center of Black communities. However, it did reinforce the sentiment that the Black church is a positive and inspiring institution. When asked their perceptions of the Black church, respondents' replies leaned toward the positive. "Safe" and "important" are among the top selections, as well as

---

[232] E. Glaude, "The Black Church Is Dead ," https://www.huffpost. com/entry/the-black-church-is-dead_b_473815.

[233] Anthea Butler, "Preaching With Power 2018 Lecture: Dr. Anthea Butler - YouTube," *Youtube*, 2017, video, https://www.youtube. com/watch?v=ve4sEnXKOyE.

"reliable" and "healing."[234] We should note "that roughly one–third tends to see the Black Church as "old–fashioned" or even "stifling," rather than "fresh" or "liberating.[235] These statistics beg the question – if a third of the Black community sees the church as old–fashioned and stifling, how can it continue to be an influential force in the Black community?

Barna stated that Black adults that find personal involvement in church desirable have declined from 90% in 1996 to 74% today. While personal involvement in church is declining, Blacks see the Black church as part of the foundation of the Black community at large. Its pastors—representatives and custodians of the institution—carry profound responsibility. The majority of religious Black adults in 2020 (69%) agree (one–third "strongly" so) that "the pastors of African American churches are the most important leaders within the Black community."[236]

The pandemic and the cries for justice came together to create the perfect storm in the Black com-

---

[234] Group B, "Most Black Adults Say Religion & the Black Experience Go Hand in Hand," https://www.barna.com/research/sobc-2/.

[235] Ibid, 4

[236] Group B, "Most Black Adults Say Religion & the Black Experience Go Hand in Hand," https://www.barna.com/research/sobc-2/.

munity. The pandemic is disproportionately affecting Black and Brown communities. The protests against racial injustice have put the community in the crosshairs of advocates of White supremacy. As corporations begin to take a stand against injustice, the Black church has been conspicuously quiet and remains on the sidelines with the exception of a few pastors. Mathis detailed the exodus of Blacks from multiracial churches because pastoral leadership will not address racism and its effects on the Black community.[237] This lack of engagement has a large "contingent of Black church members leaving their congregation to seek spiritual healing elsewhere."[238] The exodus is just not reserved for the multicultural church. The Black church "has ignored their congregation's needs in recent months, with some parishioners angered by church leaders clinging to attendance as a barometer of faithfulness even during the pandemic."[239]

The Black church is walking a very fine line in an attempt to balance rhetoric about looting and civil disobedience and preaching traditional sermons that feed the soul. Parishioners want to know that

---

[237] D. T. Mathis, "The Church's Black Exodus ," https://www. theatlantic.com/politics/archive/2020/10/why-black-parishioners-are-leaving-churches/616588/

[238] Ibid, 1

[239] Ibid, 5

their pastoral leadership will acknowledge the pain suffered due to racial injustice. They want to be understood and their concerns addressed. As a result, we are seeing declining attendance. The pandemic has allowed members to attend other churches through social media platforms that speak to their social justice ideologies.

The Barna study unearthed the fact that "Black adults are more likely to express a sense of political disempowerment than they did as recently as the mid–1990s."[240] However, church leadership has not been so willing to voice those concerns publicly. We find that congregations look to their leadership for guidance and direction in the fight against injustice, specifically racial injustice. Black pastors have been largely silent in the current activist environment, while young Black activists lead the charge. But these millennials and Generation Z members are not in the pews of Black churches. They are in the streets fighting for justice. According to Paynter, "the top causes that millennials care about are civil rights, healthcare affordability, educational access, debt relief, and

---

[240] Group B, "Most Black Adults Say Religion & the Black Experience Go Hand in Hand," https://www.barna.com/research/sobc-2/.

more equitable employment opportunities."[241] They find the Black church lacking in its enthusiasm to act.

The Black church may not be dead, but as with any organization, for it to thrive and survive, the next generations must engage the organization. According to Lipka of the Pew Research Center, 35% of adult millennials (Americans born between 1981 and 1996) are religiously unaffiliated.[242] The inability to reach Generation Y means there are fewer people to fill the pews, tithe, support missions work, and keep the church alive and open. The statistics are alarming.

- Only 2 in 10 Americans under 30 years old believe attending a church is important or worthwhile (an all–time low).

- Fifty-nine percent of millennials raised in a church have dropped out.

- Thirty-five percent of millennials have an anti–church stance, believing the church does more harm than good.

---

[241] B. Paynter, "How Millennials Are Altering the Landscape of Social Change," https://www.fastcompany.com/90381333/how-millennials-are-altering-the-landscape-of-social-change.

[242] M. Lipka, "A Closer Look at America's Rapidly Growing Religious 'nones'. ," https://www.pewresearch.org/fact-tank/2015/05/13/a-closer-look-at-americas-rapidly-growing-religious-nones/.

- Millennials are the least likely age group of anyone to attend church.[243]

The church in its current form, with its present culture, is diminishing. Those that are currently attending a church are heading for the door and changing their religious affiliation to "none." The general consensus and all analysis lead to one fact – the body of Christ is hemorrhaging members. The pews are emptying in Black churches and churches all over the world. The United States Census Bureau reported that more than 4,000 churches close their doors every year. As a result, the church cannot thrive and be successful in its mission to introduce the world to Christ, let alone tackle the injustices that our world faces today.[244]

The clash of cultures presents a perception problem for Black churches. The social agendas of many of the current activist groups do not always align with the church's beliefs. Therefore, Black churches hesitate to "endorse groups like Black Lives Matter because of ideological differences with the national organization and its founders."[245] Black parishioners

---

[243] S. Eaton, "Recklessly Alive ," http://www.recklesslyalive.com/12-reasons-millennials-are-over-church/.

[244] L. M. Dillard, "Milleneal Faith- Not Your Grandma's Church ," (2019).

[245] D. T. Mathis, "The Church's Black Exodus ," https://www.theatlantic.com/politics/archive/2020/10/why-black-parishioners-

do not necessarily agree ideologically with activist groups like BLM. Still, they identify with the struggle for justice and desire to see their church involved. This speaks to the church having to get outside the four walls. Johnson interviewed several millennials, one of which stated, "church can introduce you to spirituality, but regular attendance is not required – it's just a place."[246] Unfortunately, this is the mind-set of many millennials and Generation Z members. In talking with the youth from my church, we find they feel strongly about the community. One said, "we cringe at traditional church. We should be in the streets, out in the community." I can't say I disagree. That is the call of the church in the first place – "Go therefore and make disciples of all the nations, baptizing them in the name of the Father and of the Son and of the Holy Spirit", the operative word being "go."[247] I believe there is a place for tradition, but only if it does not get in the way of the church's stated mission – winning souls for Christ.

Young activists are frustrated that they are not listened to, and religious leadership is not partnering with them to develop strategies to combat police in-

---

are-leaving-churches/616588/
[246] R. Johnson, "Black Millennials May Be Leaving The Church, But Not the Faith," *Truth Be Told* (2019).
[247] Matthew 28:19, NKJV

justices. Butler asked, "What does it mean for clergy and millennials to act together?" Ultimately it comes down to communication and understanding how each entity operates. According Butler, millennials respond to an immediate need, an act of violence.[248] What most people see as a chaotic mass of people in the streets is an organized protest. Millennials plan to show up and show up in force. There is a level of flexibility in their strategic plan as they seize the moment – strike while the iron is hot. They will not gather at the church and listen to a sermon about the issue. They will tweet and storm Instagram, Facebook, and other social media platforms to mobilize their generation. This is about activism. Action is required. In this new era of activism, BLM may seem more influential than the Black church.

The Civil Rights Movement was birthed out of the Black church, but many of today's activist groups were birthed after the not guilty verdicts in the murders of Black men and women. The BLM movement began after a not guilty verdict was rendered in the George Zimmerman trial. A "love letter to Black people" posted on Facebook went viral, and a new civil rights movement was born. There are now over 26

---

[248] Anthea Butler, "Preaching With Power 2018 Lecture: Dr. Anthea Butler - YouTube," *Youtube*, 2017, video, https://www.youtube.com/watch?v=ve4sEnXKOyE.

BLM chapters across the United States.[249] The power of social media and this new generation of civil rights leaders will not be silenced and cannot be underestimated. For millennials, leaving the Black church allows them to become involved in activist organizations when they do not see their churches standing against injustice. The silence coming from the pulpit regarding social justice issues is deafening. Millennials expect leaders to act, not criticize every move they make. Millennials invite leaders from the "old establishment" to share their experiences, yet there is silence. There are stark differences in today's new civil rights movement. Day noted, "there are no leaders in the conventional sense: no Martin Luther King or Malcolm X, no single charismatic voice that claims to speak for the masses."[250] Those involved in the movement say this is a strength because historically, civil rights leaders have been assassinated, and they have been male.

Garza, a co–founder of BLM, addressed leadership within the organization, stating, "we have a lot of leaders, just not where you might be looking for them. If you're only looking for the straight Black

---

[249] E. Day, "#BlackLivesMatter: The Birth of a New Civil Rights Movement | Civil ..," https://www.theguardian.com/world/2015/jul/19/blacklivesmatter-birth-civil-rights-movement.
[250] Ibid, 5

man who is a preacher, you're not going to find it."[251] The new movement harnesses the localized power structure, including women and the LGBTQ community. While everyone may not agree politically, they are a powerful community that can mobilize a massive force via various social media platforms.[252]

Are these organizations perfect? Of course not. The Civil Rights Movement led by Dr. King was not perfect either. Anytime you have people coming together for a cause, several ideas and approaches are shared. Some will be accepted, and others will not. Warnock detailed the divisiveness during the rise of the Civil Rights Movement.[253] Joseph Jackson, president of the National Baptist Convention, the largest Black denomination at the time, "rejected the activist ministry of Martin Luther King, Jr., disavowing Kingian principles of civil disobedience as an appropriate Christian response."[254]Jackson believed that self-development and self-reliance would elevate Blacks versus the politics of civil disobedience. Jackson saw civil disobedience as unnecessarily divisive and disruptive to national unity. He urged African Americans to move "from protest to produc-

---

[251] Ibid

[252] Ibid

[253] Raphael G. Warnock, *The Divided Mind of the Black Church* (NYU Press, 2014).

[254] Ibid, 122

tion."[255]Jackson blamed King and his tactics of civil disobedience for the ensuing riots. Warnock stated that Jackson represented the conservative side of the Black church. He eventually ousted King from the convention.[256] Are we reliving the past? The young upstart King boldly challenged the establishment to elicit change from a nation unwilling to do so. We have come full circle. BLM and other organizations like them have a vast following that may or may not agree with the complete platform. But the part they do agree on is resistance against racial injustice. If the Black church continues to sit on the sidelines, the departure of the younger generation will become more prominent in the days, weeks, and months to come. What does the Black church do to support its members' enthusiasm to get involved and carry the mantle mandated by God? There are several areas where the church can lend its support and provide a biblical context to the long game. They include determining where there is common ground, recon-ciliation and its importance in healing and conver-sations on reparations are just a few areas the Back church can participate on a national level. The Black church must learn to use the technical tools of the day to continue pressuring the establishment into

---

[255] Ibid, 129
[256] Ibid

doing the right things. The new civil rights activism provides online pressure brought to light on a single potent issue with high visibility. The new generation of activists are young, smart, and technologically savvy. There is a restless, inventive energy to their campaigns, which can be started with little more than an iPhone.[257] Social media is an area where churches can help effectively disseminate information and develop media campaigns supporting those areas already identified as common ground.

Areas of Commonality

While the Black church may not agree with an organizations' platforms, there are areas where collaboration is possible. Jesus tells us in Matthew 12:25, "Every kingdom divided against itself is brought to desolation, and every city or house divided against itself will not stand."[258] Imagine if Black and Brown organizations, activists, and clergy worked together for one single stated purpose. A layered approach to increase engagement by Black churches has potential. While clergy work with traditional civil rights organizations like the NAACP to craft legislation, millennials march,

---

257 E. Day, "#BlackLivesMatter: The Birth of a New Civil Rights Movement | Civil ..," https://www.theguardian.com/world/2015/jul/19/blacklivesmatter-birth-civil-rights-movement.
258 Matthew 12:25, NKJV

and protest. Nothing precludes all organizations from taking a piece of the issue, one group out front, the other behind the scenes. What it takes is leaders at all levels to get over themselves. Those coming from outside a community can take a back seat to those living and working in the community. Who leads is not as important as attaining established goals and desired results. The lack of perceived support by Black clergy and churches only serves to divide the Black community. We do not have to agree with everyone on everything, but to be successful in the long term, we must determine what the common ground is and strive to hold that ground.

Reconciliation

It is never easy for two people to come together in agreement on matters such as injustice. However, it is essential that the church and activist organizations find a way to bring resources to an age-old problem. The church has a mandate in Isaiah 1:17, "Learn to do good; Seek justice, Rebuke the oppressor; Defend the fatherless, Plead for the widow."[259] The church does take its responsibility to minister to the community lightly but has recently stayed on the fringes of activism. Many activist organizations talk about reconciliation and reparations as a way to correct a

---

[259] Isaiah 1:17, NKJV

400 year wrong. The problem with this approach is that it will take the body of Christ to acknowledge the problem. Perkins defined biblical reconciliation as removing tension between parties and the restoration of a loving relationship. We are nowhere near loving one another as we listen to the racial rhetoric being turned up all over the nation. Perkins stated, "The Black church can't fix this. And the white church can't fix this. It must be the reconciled Church, Black and White Christians together imaging Christ to the world."[260] Is racial reconciliation even possible? How do we bring together organizations with deep-seated biases and, many times, pure hate that do not want to give up their privilege? Any wall that we build based on racism and hatred can be torn down. We have to be intentional about doing the work to build bridges and doors for our fellow man to walk through.[261]

So many times in my Army career, I heard, "I don't see color, I see green." Morrison pointed out that in Galatians 3:26–29, Paul emphasized that unity can be found in diversity.[262] That there is no Jew, Gentile, neither slave nor free, nor is there male or female. We are all one in Jesus Christ. This is what the Black

---

[260] John Perkins, *One Blood* (Moody Publishers, 2018).
[261] Latasha Morrison, *Be the Bridge* (WaterBrook, 2019).
[262] Ibid

church should be preaching, teaching, and demonstrating. When we say we do not see color, or we say we are color blind, we diminish God's image in each of us. If you do not see color, then you do not see me.

For centuries the Bible has been used to enslave and abuse the people of God. Is it not time we interpret the Word of God in proper context? We must remove the blinders that keep us from acknowledging foundational truths. Let's start with this one. Race, as we know it, is a political and social construct created by man to assert power and maintain a hierarchy.[263] When society takes a stand against the injustices perpetrated due to racism, it no longer becomes profitable, and change will occur.

Looking across the political landscape today, Major League Baseball's decision to change venues as a result of racist voting legislation in Georgia is a start in acknowledging the long-standing injustices in the state of Georgia. The Black church must be vocal and mobilize in support of any business that takes a stand. We know the economics of this situation will disproportionately affect Black and Brown communities. Church's should anticipate the needs that will arise as corporate America makes decisions about its level of support for racial justice. Again these are long-term strategies that should be discussed among civil

---

[263] Ibid

rights groups. Sometimes the only way to change minds is to affect the bottom line. When injustice no longer becomes profitable, change will occur.

Reparations

Reparation is the "making of amends for a wrong one has done by paying money or otherwise helping those who have been wronged."[264] Any conversation about reparations tends to start with, "why should I pay for something I had nothing to do with?" But reparation is a biblical concept. Exodus 22:1, 3–6, and 14 detail what was required under the Mosaic law to pay restitution for particular instances.[265]

> If a man steals an ox or a sheep, and slaughters it or sells it, he shall restore five oxen for an ox and four sheep for a sheep.[266] If the sun has risen on him, there shall be guilt for his bloodshed. He should make full restitution; if he has nothing, he shall be sold for his theft. If the theft is indeed found alive in his hand, whether it is an ox or donkey or sheep, he shall restore double.

---

[264] N. Davis, "Asheville Reparations Resolution Is Designed to Provide Black ..," accessed May 23, 2023, https://www.ashevillenc.gov/news/asheville-reparations-resolution-is-designed-to-help-black-community-access-to-the-opportunity-to-build-wealth/.

[265]

[266] Exodus 22:1, NKJV

> If a man causes a field or vineyard to be grazed, and lets loose his animal, and it feeds in another man's field, he shall make restitution from the best of his field and the best of his vineyard. If a fire breaks out and catches in thorns, so that stacked grain, standing grain, or the field is consumed, he who kindled the fire shall surely make restitution.[267]

> And if a man borrows *anything* from his neighbor, and it becomes injured or dies, the owner of it not *being* with it, he shall surely make *it* good.[268]

In the New Testament, Zacchaeus, a tax collector, cheated the people for some time. According to Luke 19:8, Zacchaeus repented and made restitution. He told Jesus, "look, Lord, I give half of my goods to the poor; and if I have taken anything from anyone by false accusation, I restore fourfold."[269] There are many reasons why reparations have been a hard sell in Congress. However, there are city councils that are exploring the possibilities.

In the United States, reparations would acknowledge the wrongdoing over 400 plus years of systematic racism and hate. On July 14, 2020, Ashville, North

---

267 Exodus 22:3–6, NKJV
268 Exodus 22:14, NKJV
269 Luke 19:8, NKJV

Carolina City Council unanimously passed a resolution supporting community reparations for Black Asheville. The resolution acknowledged systemic racism present in the community, as well as nationally. The resolution was put in place to atone for the price of slave labor or racist policies that resulted in a loss of equity, opportunity, and assets.[270] The community will allocate $1 million in reparations to the Black community.

Churches are making a move to embrace reparations as well. ABC News reported in December 2020:

> Episcopal Church has been the most active major denomination thus far. Others, including the United Methodist Church and the Evangelical Lutheran Church of America, are urging congregations to consider similar steps. The Roman Catholic Church and the Southern Baptist Convention have not embraced reparations as official policy.[271]

---

[270] N. Davis, "Asheville Reparations Resolution Is Designed to Provide Black ..," accessed May 23, 2023, https://www.ashevillenc.gov/news/asheville-reparations-resolution-is-designed-to-help-black-community-access-to-the-opportunity-to-build-wealth/.

[271] D. Crary, "More US Churches Commit to Racism-Linked Reparations," accessed May 29, 2023, : https://abcnews.go.com/US/wireStory/us-churches-commit-racism-linked-reparations-74701219.

Perkins worked with community development organizations to help communities work together to balance some of the inequities of life. Perkins stated that reconciliation is a God issue, and the lack of reconciliation is because "we've not been able to arrive at the solution because we haven't seen or acknowledged the problem." [272]

Truth and Reconciliation Commission - How to Forgive

Tutu stated, "Forgiveness is not just personally rewarding. It's also a political necessity."[273] South Africa transitioned from apartheid to a democracy. Much like America after the civil war. Tutu realized the country had to embrace the biblical principle and commandment to love your neighbor. Friends and enemies alike. Tutu stated, "True reconciliation is based on forgiveness, and forgiveness is based on true confession, and confession is based on penitence, on contrition, on sorrow for what you have done."[274] The Truth and Reconciliation Commission, founded by Nelson Mandela in 1995, was created to investigate gross human rights violations perpetrated during the Apartheid regime from 1960 to 1994,

---

[272] John Perkins, *One Blood* (Moody Publishers, 2018).

[273] D. Tutu, "Truth and Reconciliation | Greater Good," accessed May 23, 2023, https://greatergood.berkeley.edu/article/item/truth_and_reconciliation.

[274] Ibid

including abductions, killings, and torture. Its mandate covered transgressions by both the state and the liberation movements. It allowed the commission to hold special hearings focused on specific sectors, institutions, and individuals. Controversially the TRC was empowered to grant amnesty to perpetrators who confessed their crimes truthfully and completely to the commission.[275] It is interesting to note that of the 7,000 applications requesting amnesty, only 849 were granted. Yet, the process of truthful confrontation facilitated the healing of a nation.

The wounds of America continue to reopen with every White supremacist rant. A nation continues to disenfranchise Black and Brown people as voting laws are changed. This nation has gone through several civil rights movements to establish what should have been enacted upon at the founding of this nation. "We hold these truths to be self–evident, that all men are created equal, that they are endowed by their Creator with certain unalienable rights that among these are life, liberty and the pursuit of happiness."[276]

---

[275] "United States Institute of Peace," https://www.usip.org/.

[276] Thomas Jefferson, "Declaration of Independence: A Transcription | National Archives," https://www.archives.gov/founding-docs/declaration-transcript.

I started this book by saying I could be an angry Black woman but for God's grace. Make no mistake; God will judge us all in due time. But what do we do until then? Paul tells us in Ephesians 4:26,"be angry, and do not sin": do not let the sun go down on your wrath."[277] There are constructive uses for that anger. The Black church must engage. It has the mandate to do so. The church cannot continue to sit on the sidelines in silence. While there are a few that believe the Black church is dead in its present state, Warnock told us, "Concern over its prospects for resuscitation and role as an instrument of liberation is very much alive."[278] God is justice. Therefore, the Black church must be about justice as well. A new generation is rising, and they need guidance and support. The Black church has a critical role in influencing and participating in solving the injustices perpetrated on Black and Brown communities. There are several ways to confront the issues. However the Lord leads you to help in the fight against injustice, be bold in your approach. Remember, leadership is about influence. Black church, rise and take your rightful place! It's time to get into "good trouble."

---

[277] Ephesians 4:26, NKJV

[278] Raphael G. Warnock, *The Divided Mind of the Black Church* (NYU Press, 2014)

Key Takeaways

- The Black Church is not dead. Of course, there are challenges that we must address, but the black church is not dead. Just because she is not leading the current charge does not mean she is not involved behind the scenes. Congregants believe the black church is influential in the community. The question is how to organize and mobilize with the rising tide of dissent across the nation, not to respond violently but *biblically*.

- God is Justice. It may seem obvious, but the black church has the mandate to do what is morally right. Sitting on the sidelines has never been an option.

- The method and the organizations many are using or joining to protest and dismantle unjust systems do not align with the church's values. As a result, there is division and numerous disconnects within the black community. A divided house cannot stand.[279]

- The Black Church, while influential, is seen as old-fashioned, stifling, and, for many hypocritical. Leaders must change this perception by incorporating the views of a new generation. Church, as usual, will not survive.

---

[279] Matthew 12:25, NKJV

Questions for Reflection and Discussion

1. How are you bridging the gap between generations, organizations, etc.?

____

____

____

____

2. What is your vision for social reform involvement? Does it align biblically?

____

____

____

____

3. God's message never changes. Are you changing the method to reach the masses?

____

____

____

____

FINAL THOUGHTS

The Black church is not dead. She has just been silent. Now is the time for her to speak. It is not a matter of political or social will. It is God's will. God never intended for the church to sit idly by and allow society to misuse and abuse His people. The day of reckoning is upon us. God will judge our actions or inaction. The Fordham panel met in 2017 and posited, "has America lost its moral center?"[280] The answer was a resounding yes, but there is hope. God called the church to love and care for the people. If we are not demonstrating love and being a voice for the disenfranchised, we are complicit in supporting the whims of a society that has lost its moral center.

I have shown that God does not forget his people. It may not be on the timeline we want or expect, but justice will prevail. We must accept the call to stand in the gap for those that cannot stand for

---

[280] P. Feuerherd, "Has America Lost it's Moral Center?," https://www.ncronline.org/news/politics/has-america-lost-its-moral-center-asks-fordham-panel.

themselves. Justice is a heart issue. The church must help change hearts. If we do our part, God always does his. For Dr. King's dream to become a reality, the church must be the nation's conscience. Otherwise, no change will last, and people will continue to suffer.

We may not be slaves living on a plantation picking cotton or tobacco anymore, but the giants of injustice, hatred, racism still prevail. When we do not engage in or initiate the conversation, we become slaves to our silence. We must examine ourselves. We cannot be deceived into believing there is no role for the Black church in today's fight for justice. We cannot turn a blind eye to the problems plaguing our communities today.

For Dr. King's dream to become a reality, the church must be the nation's conscience and speak out. Society will put forth many that will say "change will not happen" or "it cannot be done." All of the leaders we have explored accepted the call against unimaginable odds. They all believed there was something they could do. With no regard for personal safety, all these leaders demonstrated that the cost of doing nothing paled in comparison to the cost of standing for what is right. The bloodhounds of racism and hate have been loosed yet again. We must not run and hide, but we must call these injustices out wherever they appear! The constitution has not changed, we are free to speak, free to protest, free to defend our inalienable rights as Americans, but we have become comfortable, complacent, and in some cases complicit.

There is a new generation of activists rising to fight against injustice. It was the Black church that stood and said, "not on my watch," not so many years ago. We, the people, are the church, not the edifices we have built with the coffee bar and the nice parking lot. There is a role for the Black church in social justice reform. Now is the time for her to speak. Biblical justice is what we seek. It is not a matter of political or social will. It is God's will.

REFERENCES

Acharya, A., Blackwell, M., & Sen, M. (2016). The political legacy of American slavery. *The Journal of Politics, 78*(3), 621–641. https://www.journals.uchicago.edu/doi/abs/10.1086/686631 Acharya, A., Blackwell, M., & Sen, M. (2014, November 16). The Political Legacy of American Slavery. Standford, CA, USA.

Adamo, D. (2018). A Silent Unheard Voice in the Old Testament: The Cushite Woman Whom Moses Married in Number 12:1-10. *In die Skriflig*, 1-8.

Adamo, D. T. (2017). *The Burning Bush (Ex 3:1-6): A Study of Natural Phenomena as Manisfestation of Divine Presence in the Old Testament and in African Context.* Retrieved from HTS Teologiese Studies/Theological Studies: https://doi.org/10.4102/hts.v73i3.4576

Africa, T. C. (1995). *Truth Commission: COmmission of Truth and Reconciliation.* Washington D. C.: United States Institute of Peace.

Alexander, M. (2010). *The New Jim Crow.* New York: The New Press.

Allen, D. S. (2020). *Why Social Justice is Not Biblical Justice.* Grand Rapids: Credo House Publishers.

Ayers, D. L. (2013). *To serve this present age: Social justice ministries and the Black church.* New Jersey: Judson Press, Kindle Edition.

Ayers, M. (2015). *Power to Lead: Five Essentials for the Practice of Biblical Leadership.* Spring: RBK Publishing (Kindle Edition).

Bankston, C. L. (2010). Social Justice: Cultural Origins of a Perspective Theory. *The Independent Review, vol 15, number 2 Fall 2010*, 165-178.

Barker, R. L. (2003). *The Social Work Dictionary*. Washington DC: NASW Press.

Baucham , Voddie. "Biblical Justice Vs. Social Justice | Voddie Baucham - YouTube." *Biblical Justice Vs Social Justice* , 2021. Video, https://www.youtube.com/watch?v=i60eQZPG5XM.

Baudot, J. (2006). The International Forum for Social Development (Economic and Social Affairs). *Social Justice in an Open World - The Role of the United Nations* (pp. 1-146). New York: United Nations.

Bayes, R. (2015). *A Biblical View of Disability*. Retrieved from Be Thinking Org: https://www.bethinking.org/human-life/a-biblical-view-of-disability

Beisner, C. E. (2013). *Social Justice: How Good Intentions Undermine Justice and Gospel*. United States: Family Research Council.

Berger, R. M. (2007). What the Heck is 'Social Justice'? *Sojourners*, 37.

Billingsley, A. (1999). *Mighty Like a River: The Black Church and Social Reform*. New York: Oxford Press.

Brenner, A. (1993). *Introduction: A Feminist Companion to Judges*. Sheffield: Sheffield Academic Press.

Butler, A. (2018, March 29). *Preaching With Power 2018 Lecture: Millennials, Social Justice and the Future of Religious Advocacy in America*. Retrieved from https://www.youtube.com/watch?v=ve4sEnXKOyE

Carter, J. (2018, August 17). *The FAQs: What Christians Should Know About Social Justice*. Retrieved from The Gospel Coalition: https://www.thegospelcoalition.org/article/faqs-christians-know-social-justice/

Chappelow, J. (2020, Sep 30). *Social Justice.* Retrieved from Investopedia: https://www.investopediaco.aspm/terms/s/social-justice.asp

Clark, J. I. (2014). *SOCIAL JUSTICE AND BLACK CHURCH LEADERSHIP: A PHENOMENOLOGICAL STUDY.* Ann Arbor: Proquest LLC.

Cole, L. G. (1974). *The Samaritans: A Yesterday People Today.* Retrieved from Church of Jesus Christ: churchofjesuschrist.org

Cone, J. H. (1969). *Black theology and Black power.* New York: The Seabury Press.

Cone, J. H., & Wilmore, G. S. (1979). *Black Theology: A Documentary History: 1966-1979.* Maryknoll: Orbis Books.

Craig, G. (2002). Poverty, social work and social justice. *British Journal of Social Work, Volume 32, Issue 6,* 669-682.

Crary, D. (2020, December 13). *More US Churches Commit to Racism-linked Reparations.* Retrieved from ABC News: https://abcnews.go.com/US/wireStory/us-churches-commit-racism-linked-reparations-74701219

Creswell, J. W. (2014). *Research Design.* Thousand Oaks: Sage Publishing.

Dahl, N. (1974). Nations in the New Testament. *New Testament Christianity for Africa and the World: Essays in Honour of Harry Sawyerr,* 54-68.

Davis, N. (2020, July 20). *Asheville reparations resolution is designed to provide Black community access to the opportunity to build wealth.* Retrieved from The City of Asheville: https://www.ashevillenc.gov/news/asheville-reparations-resolution-is-designed-to-help-black-community-access-to-the-opportunity-to-build-wealth/

Davis, S. G. (2019, March 18). *Esther Position Power Person Power, Gifts.* Retrieved from God Gifts You Calling and Purpose: https://godgiftsyou.com/blog/2019/3/13/calling-and-purpose-8estherposition-power-personal-power-gifts.

Day, E. (2015, July 19). *#BlackLivesMatter: the birth of a new civil rights movement.* Retrieved from The Guardian: https://www.theguardian.com/world/2015/jul/19/blacklivesmatter-birth-civil-rights-movement

Deffinbaugh, R. L. (2007). *David's Youth: A Training Ground for Godly Leadership.* Retrieved from Bible.Org: https://bible.org/seriespage/1-davids-youth-training-ground-godly-leadership,

DeLong, D. P. (1996). Woman and Culture in the New Testament World. *Leaven,* 24-28.

Dictionary, O. A. (2005). *Oxford Advanced American Dictionary 7th Ed.* Oxford Advanced American Dictionary.

Dillard, L. M. (2019). Millinneal Faith - Not Your Grandma's Church.

Dionigi, F., & Kleidosty, J. (2017). *An Analysis of John Rawls's A Theory of Justice.* London: Macat International.

Du Bois, W. (1903). *The Souls of Black Folk.* Tampa: Millennium Publications.

Du Bois, W. E. (1903). *Ths Souls of Black Folks.* The Project Gutenberg EBook.

Dutton, T. A. (2007). Colony Over-the-Rhin. *The Black Scholar, Vol 37, Number 3,* 14-27.

Eaton, S. (2016). *Recklessly Alive.* Retrieved July 22, 2018, from http://www.recklesslyalive.com/12-reasons-millennials-are-over-church/

Eberling, J. R. (2010). *Women's Lives in the Biblical Times.* New York: T & T Clark International.

Eck, D. L. (2001). *A New Religious America: How a "Christin Country" Has Become the World's Most Religiously Diverse Nation.* New York: HarperCollins e-books.

Encyclopedia, J. (1906). *Jewish Encyclopedia.*

Evans, T. (2019). *The Tony Evans Study Bible.* Nashville: Holman Bible Publishers.

Feuerherd, P. (2017, December 5). *Has America lost it's moral center?* Retrieved from National Catholic Reporter: https://www.ncronline.org/news/politics/has-america-lost-its-moral-center-asks-fordham-panel

Gardner, H. (1983). *Frames of Mind: The Theory of Multiple Intelligences.* New York: Basic Books.

Gates, H. L. (2021, February 17). *To Understand America, You Need to Understand the Black Church.* Retrieved from Time: https://time.com/5939921/henry-lous-gates-american-history-black-church/

Glaser, Z. (2020, July 30). *The Role of Women in the Bible.* Retrieved from Jews for Jesus: https://jewsforjesus.org/publications/newsletter/newsletter-jun-1988/the-role-of-women-in-the-bible/

Glaude, E. (2010, April 26). *The Black Church is Dead.* Retrieved from Huffington Post: https://www.huffpost.com/entry/the-black-church-is-dead_b_473815

Grandison, T. (2016, August 26). *The Root Cause Sustaining Injustice.* Retrieved from https://tyronegrandison.medium.com/the-root-cause-sustaining-injustice-d5b7ae5eee1,

Grant, E. I. (2016, September 14). *The History of the Black Church.* Retrieved from The Witness: https://thewitnessbcc.com/history-black-church/

Group, B. (2021, February 18). *Most Black Adults Say Religion & the Black Experience Go Hand in Hand.* Retrieved from Barna: https://www.barna.com/research/sobc-2/

Guzik, D. (2018). *Acts 9 - The conversion of Saul of Tarsus.* Retrieved from Enduring Word: https://enduringword.com/bible-commentary/acts-9/

Guzik, D. (2018a). *David at the Adullam Cave, Saul Murders the Priests.* Retrieved from Enduring Word: https://enduringword.com/bible-commentary/1%20Samuel%2022/

Guzik, D. (2018b). *Esther 3 - Haman's Conspiracy.* Retrieved from Enduring Word: https://enduringword.com/bible-commentary/esther-3/

Guzik, D. (2018c). *Esther 7-Haman's End.* Retrieved from Endurikng Word: https://enduringword.com/bible-commentary/esther-7/

Guzik, D. (2018d). *John 4 - A Samaritan Woman and a Nobleman Meet Jesus.* Retrieved from Enduring Word: https://enduringword.com/bible-commentary/john-4/

Guzik, D. (2020). *Exodus 7 - Miracles and Plagues Before Pharoah.* Retrieved from Enduring Word: https://enduringword.com/bible-commentary/exodus-7/

Henning, M. (2019). *Disabilities in the Bible.* Retrieved from Bible Odyssey: http://bibleodyssey.org/en/people/related-articles/disabilities-in-the-bible

Hudson, K. D. (2017). With Equality and Opportunity for All? Emerging Scholars Define Social Justice for Social Work. *British Journal of Social Work, Volume 47, Issue 7,* 1959-1978.

Humphreys, C. J. (1998). The Number of People in the Exodus from Egypt: Decoding Mathematically the Very Large Numbers in Numbers I and XXI. *Vetus Testamentum,* 200.

Institute, B. o. (2020). *Founding Principles and Virtues.* Retrieved from Bill of Rights Institute: https://billofrightsinstitute.org/founding-documents/founding-principles/

Jefferson, T. (1776, July 4). *America's Founding Documents.* Retrieved from National Archives: https://www.archives.gov/founding-docs/declaration-transcript

Johnson, R. (2019, November 11). *Black Millennials May be Leaving The Church, But Not the Faith.* Retrieved from Truth Be Told: https://truthbetold.news/2019/11/black-millennials-may-be-leaving-the-church-but-not-the-faith/

Khalifa, H. O. (2017, October). *IPL.* Retrieved from Social Justice in Education: A literature Review: IPL.org

King, M. L. (1957, November 17). *Loving Your Enemies.* Retrieved from MLK Online: http://www.mlkonline.net/enemies.html

King, M. L. (1957). Nonviolence and Racial Justice. *Christian Century*, 165-167.

King, M. L. (1963, April 16). *Letter From Birmingham Jail.* Retrieved from Liberation Curriculum: www.liberationcurriculum.org

Kranz, J. (2020, June 19). *Oppression and Social Justice in the Bible: A Beginner's Guide.* Retrieved from Beginner's Guide to the Bible: https://overviewbible.com/oppression/

Lane, M. (2018). Ancient Political Philosophy. In E. N. Zalta, *The Stanford Encyclopedia of Philosophy.* Stanford: Metaphysics Research Lab, Stanford University.

Limbaugh, D. (2018, October 25). *Why Did God Choose the Apostle Paul?* Retrieved from The Spectrum: https://www.thespectrum.com/story/opinion/2018/10/25/why-did-god-choose-apostle-paul/1767491002/

Lincoln, E. (1977). *The Black Church Since Fraxier.* New York: Schocken Books.

Lincoln, E. C., & Mamiya, L. H. (1990). *The Black Church in the African American Experience.* Duke University Press.

Lincoln, E. C., & Mamiya, L. H. (2003). *The Black Church in the African American Experience.* Durham: Duke University Press [Kindle version].

Lipka, M. (2015, May 13). *A closer look at America's rapidly growing religious 'nones'.* Retrieved from Pew Research Center: https://www.pewresearch.org/fact-tank/2015/05/13/a-closer-look-at-americas-rapidly-growing-religious-nones/

Lockyer. (1988). *Chapter 3. Nameless Bible Women.* Retrieved from All The Women of the Bible: https://www.biblegateway.com/resources/all-women-bible/Chapter-3-Nameless-Bible-Women

Lowe, J. S., & Shipp, S. C. (2014). Black Church and Black College Community Development Corporations: Enhancing the Public Sector Discourse. *The Western Journal of Black Studies, Volume 38, Number 4, 244-259.*

Mathis, D. T. (2020, October 11). *The Church's Black Exodus.* Retrieved from The Atlantic: https://www.theatlantic.com/politics/archive/2020/10/why-black-parishioners-are-leaving-churches/616588/

Maxwell, J. C. (2002). *Leadership 101.* Nashville: Harper Collins.

Maxwell, J. C. (2007). *Maxwell Leadership Bible.* Nashville: Thomas Nelson.

Maxwell, J. C. (2007). *The 21 Irrefutable Laws of Leadership.* HarperCollins.

Mayerstein, M. A. (2018). *The Book of Esther - Salvation from Genocide.* Seattle: On-Demand Publishing, LLC.

McKinney, R. I. (1971). The Black Church: Its Development and Present Impact. *The Harvard Theological Review, Volume 64, Issue 4, 452-481.*

McMickle, M. A. (2020, November 1). *The Black Church in America - A Brief History.* Retrieved from African American Registry: https://aaregistry.org/story/the-black-church-a-brief-history/

Merrett, C. D. (2004). Social Justice: What is it? WHy Teach It? *Journal of Geography, Volume 103, Issue 3, 93-101.*

Metzger, P. L. (2010). *What is Biblical Justice.* Retrieved from Christianity Today: https://www.christianitytoday.com/pastors/2010/summer/biblicaljustice.html

Mole, G. D. (2011). Cruel Justice, Responsibilitym and Forgiveness: On Levinas's Reading of the Gibeonites. *The Author, 253-271.*

Morrison, L. (2019). *Be The Bridge - Pursuing God's Heart for Racial Reconciliation.* Carol Stream: Crown Publishing Group.

Munroe, M. (2011). *Understanding Your Place in God's Kingdom.* Shippensburg: Destiny Image Publishers.

Northouse, P. (2016). *Leadership Theory and Practice.* Thousand Oaks: Sage.

Ornstein, A. C. (2017). Social Justice: History, Purpose and Meaning. *Social Science and Public Policy, Volume 54*, 541-548.

Otieno, P. A. (2009). Biblical and Theological Perspectives on Disability: Implications on the Rights of Persons with Disability in Kenya. *Disability Studies Quarterly*.

Pattillo-McCoy, M. (1998). Church Culture as a Strategy of Action in the Black Community. *American Sociological Review, Volume 63, Number 6*, 767-784.

Paynter, B. (2019, July 26). *How millennials are altering the landscape of social change.* Retrieved from Fast Company: https://www.fastcompany.com/90381333/how-millennials-are-altering-the-landscape-of-social-change

Perkins, J. (2018). *Parting Words to the Church on Race and Love - One Blood.* Chicago: Moody Publishers.

Piper, J. (2012, February 21). *Why Did God Let Paul Become a Murderer?* Retrieved from Desiring God: https://www.desiringgod.org/articles/why-did-god-let-paul-become-a-murderer

Pipkin, C. W. (1925). The Ideal of Social Justice. *The Southwestern Political and Social Science Quarterly*, 201-202.

Reisch, M. (2002). Defining Social Justice in a Socially Unjust World. *Families in Society: The Journal of Contemporary Human Services, Volume 83, Number 4*, 343-354.

Retief, F. P., Cilliers, J., & Riekert, S. (2005). Eunuchs in the Bible. *Acta Theolgica*, 247-258.

Schipper, J. (2006). *Disability Studies and the Hebrew Bible: Figuring Mephibosheth in the David Story.* New York: T & T Clark.

Scorgie, G. G. (2011). *Dictionary of Christian Spirituality.* Grand Rapids: Zondervan.

Setzer, C. (2019). *The Syrophoenician Woman.* Retrieved from Bible Odyssey: https://www.bibleodyssey.org:443/en/people/related-articles/syrophoenician-woman

Sherriff, G. (2018, December 6). *Letter from Birmingham Jail.* Retrieved from LitCharts.

Smith, C. (2014, Fbruary 3). *Paul and Leadership.* Retrieved from The Briefing: thebriefing.com.au/2014/02/paul-and-leadership/

Stewart, D. T. (2008). A Review of Disability Studies and the Hebrew Bible: Figuring Mephibosheth in the David Story. *Disability in the Hebrew Bible*, 89-90.

Stott, J. (2013, December 16). *Culture and the Bible.* Retrieved from Intervarsity: https://ism.intervarsity.org/resource/culture-and-bible

Taylor, A. (2012, February 20). *World Vision.* Retrieved from What does social justice really mean?: https://www.worldvision.org/blog/social-justice-really-mean#:~:text=The%20Bible%20makes%20social%20justice,disinherited%20%E2%80%94%20you%20get%20my%20point.

"The Terminator (1984) Official Trailer - YouTube." *The Terminator*, 1984. Video, https://www.youtube.com/watch?v=k64P4l2W-meg.

Tisby, J. (2019). *The Color of Compromise.* Grand Rapids: Zondervan.

Trible, P. (1984). *Text of Terror: Literary Feminist Readings of Biblical Narrative.* Philadelphia: Fortress.

Tripp, P. D. (2020). *Lead.* Wheaton: Crossway.

Tutu, D. (2004, September 1). *Truth and Reconciliation.* Retrieved from Greater Good Magazine: https://greatergood.berkeley.edu/article/item/truth_and_reconciliation

Waggoner, S. E. (2017). *Normal is not biblical: An explaratory study of ministry with developmental diabilities in the Arkansas Conference of the United Methodist Church.* Retrieved from Pro Quest: http://eres.regent.edu/login?url=https://www-proquest-com.ezproxy.regent.edu/dissertations-theses/normal-is-not-biblical-exploratory-study-ministry/docview/1950091548/se-2?accountid=13479

Wakefield, J. (1998). Psychotherapy, Distributive Justice and Social Work Revisited. *Smith College Studies in Social Work, Volume 69, Issue 1*, 25-57.

Wallis, J. (2016). *America's Original Sin - Racisim, White Privilege and the Bridge to a New America*. Grand Rapids: Brazos Press.

Warnock, R. G. (2014). *The Divided Mind of the Black Church (Religion, Race, and Ethnicity)*. New York: New York University Press.

West, J. (2016, September 25). *Profile of a Religious Terrorist*. Retrieved from Colonial Presbyterian Church: https://www.colonialkc.org/sermon-media/2016manuscripts/saul-the-profile-of-a-religious-terrorist/

Winston, B. E., & Patterson, K. (2006). An Integrative Definition of Leadership. *International Journal of Leadership Studies*, 6-66.

CONCISE
Publishing

DELIVERANCE
FOR
REAL

Dr. Shirley R. Brown, Th.D

WORKBOOK